A Child Is Born

A Child Is Born

W. JEFFREY MARSH

CFI
Springville, Utah

ISBN 13: 978-1-59955-183-8

Published by CFI, an imprint of Cedar Fort, Inc., 2373 W. 700 S., Springville, UT 84663
Distributed by Cedar Fort, Inc., www.cedarfort.com

LIBRARY OF CONGRESS CATALOGING-IN-PUBLICATION DATA

Marsh, W. Jeffrey.
  [Unto us a child is born]
  A child is born / W. Jeffrey Marsh.
    p. cm.
  Includes index.
  Originally published: Unto us a child is born. Salt Lake City, Utah :
Bookcraft, c1994.
  ISBN 978-1-59955-183-8 (alk. paper)
  1. Jesus Christ—Nativity. 2. Jesus Christ—Mormon interpretations. I.
Title.

  BX8643.J4M27 2008
  232.92—dc22

                    2008014586

Cover design by Nicole Williams
Cover design © 2008 by Lyle Mortimer
Edited and typeset by Kimiko M. Hammari

Printed in the United States of America

10 9 8 7 6 5 4 3 2 1

Printed on acid-free paper

To my children and grandchildren.
Merry Christmas!

CONTENTS

ONE
Why Christmas Is So Exceptional . . . 1

TWO
Christ's Birth—The Centerpiece of Christmas . . . 5

THREE
Symbolism vs. Commercialism . . . 13

FOUR
"Faithful Witnesses Whom I have Chosen" . . . 27

FIVE
"Unto Us a Child Is Born" . . . 41

SIX
"Five Years More . . . Then Cometh the Son of God" . . . 45

SEVEN
The Forerunner Who Prepared the Way . . . 55

EIGHT
The Glorious Announcement to Mary . . . 63

NINE
The Birth of John the Baptist . . . 75

TEN
The Days Were Accomplished That She Should Be Delivered . . . 81

ELEVEN

Events in the Ancient Americas the Day Before Christ Was Born . . . 87

TWELVE

The Birth of the Messiah . . . 95

THIRTEEN

While Shepherds Watched . . . 103

FOURTEEN

"Mine Eyes Have Seen" . . . 115

FIFTEEN

Jesus' Youth—A Time of Preparation . . . 125

SIXTEEN

Wise Men and Wise Women Still Seek Him . . . 133

SEVENTEEN

"Maybe Christmas Doesn't Come from a Store" . . . 139

APPENDIX

A Family Christmas Nativity . . . 153

INDEX . . . 159

ONE

Why Christmas Is So Exceptional

WHENEVER GOD HAS AN IMPORTANT mission to fulfill, He sends a child to earth who, with great faith and effort, will accomplish the seemingly impossible. When an entire community needed to be prepared to be translated and lifted up into the presence of God, Enoch was born (Moses 7:16–19). When a nation stood in desperate need to be saved from treachery and annihilation, Esther was born (Esther 4:13–14). At another time, on another continent, God raised up an army of stripling warriors whose mothers instilled such unwavering faith in their hearts that they rose up and rescued their nation from destruction (Alma 56:46–48, 55–56). And when God was ready to send His Only Begotten Son to earth—whose sacrifice in Gethsemane and Golgotha, and whose resurrection from the Garden Tomb would forever open the door for the immortality and eternal life of all His children— God sent a forerunner to prepare the way, a child later known as John the Baptist (JST, John 1:1–34; JST Appendix).

But of all the billions of children born to this earth, the Babe of Bethlehem born to Mary was unique. No one else's birth was like His. No one else was like Him. He not only stood preeminent above all others (Abraham 3:19), but He was also very different from everyone else. He was half mortal and half eternal. His birth was so distinctive and exceptional that forever afterward, time would be marked by it because it would forever change the fate of mankind. Most nations around the world celebrate the event. And in a future day, every knee will bow before Him and confess that He is Jesus the Christ, the Savior and Redeemer of all mankind (Mosiah 27:31). Christ's birth is the reason for the Christmas season!

Jesus Christ was not merely a great moral teacher, or a gifted leader, or one of a number of the prophets. He was unlike every person ever born. The Savior declared that "the Father hath sent me" (John 5:36). His life was a specific and foreordained mission to help everyone else. C. S. Lewis described how belief in Christ as the Savior of mankind is a do-or-die proposition. There is no middle ground on this issue—either He is the Redeemer of all mankind, or He is not:

> This man was, and is, the Son of God, or else a madman or something worse. . . . But don't let us come with any patronizing nonsense about his being a great human teacher. He has not left that open to us. . . . I'm trying here to prevent anyone from saying that really silly thing that people often say about Him: "I'm ready to accept Jesus as a great moral teacher, but I don't accept His claim to be a God." That is the thing we must not say. A man who was merely a man and said the sort of things Jesus said, would not be a great moral teacher. He'd be either a lunatic—on the level with the man who says he's a poached egg—or else he'd be the Devil of Hell.[1]

The Savior's life and mission are real, and an awareness of His divinity is gathering steam across the earth to prepare the world for His Second Coming. There is a special spirit that envelops the earth at Christmastime. It's a miracle, just like His life, His mission, His character, and His caring.

This book is about the greatest Christmas miracle—the divine birth of the one and only person who can stop wars, bring peace to the Middle East, put down all false doctrine, breathe new life into marriages and family relations, solve global warming, make the environment pristine, bring this earth into a paradisiacal state, and deliver this earth, and all its righteous inhabitants who are destined to inherit it forever, back into the presence of God, where there will be no more tears but only happiness, peace, rest from every trouble, all cares, and all sorrow. That's going to take a miracle, and Jesus Christ's miraculous birth makes it all possible.

Isaiah described this Christmas miracle with picture-perfect prose: "For unto us a child is born, unto us a son is given: and the government shall be upon his shoulder: and his name shall be called Wonderful Counselor, The mighty God, The everlasting Father, The Prince of Peace" (Isaiah 9:6; punctuation altered).

I extend heartfelt thanks to wonderful parents and grandparents who have blessed my life with so many great Christmas memories and traditions. They sacrificed much to make Christmas a marvelous and magical time of year. May the December joys our parents created for us each Christmas become like a storehouse of memories that will warm us in the Decembers of our lives.

Every December I make a special effort to teach the true story of Christmas, as found in the scriptures. The age-old story takes on new life and meaning when it is read in sequence, interwoven with the revelatory insights found in the Joseph Smith Translation, coupled with the commentaries from modern prophets. We wish we could have been there with Christ in Jerusalem to thank Him, to follow Him. And we can! Not physically, of course, but spiritually we can journey to Bethlehem with Joseph and Mary, sit with shepherds who heard angelic choirs, watch the faithfulness of those in ancient America the night before He was born, travel with the wise men who came seeking the infant-king, and ponder with Mary the incredible experiences she kept in her heart—because we have the scriptures! If we, like the wise men, will search for Christ by reading and pondering the scriptures, we can find Him at Christmastime. Unlike the innkeeper, however, we need to let Him in. "Where meek souls will receive Him still, the dear Christ enters in."

As a parent, I've been concerned about the increasing commercialism during the holidays. The secular swamp is steadily growing and swallowing too many sacred things. I wanted my children and grandchildren to be able to enjoy the real story of what Christmas is all about. I also wanted them to enjoy every symbol associated with this holiday, but also have the ability to look beyond the symbols and comprehend the great realities they represent. This book is my attempt to share with them some of the feelings I have for the Savior and why His birth and ministry on this earth are so important. He is the light and the life of the world.

The most profound insights expressed in this work come from modern prophets whose inspired teachings help us better understand the writings of ancient prophets. Prophets interpret prophets, as is their right, and our blessing. With gratitude I acknowledge all the prophets over the centuries, including the present one, who have carefully recorded their testimonies of Christ's life, and preserved the words of His ministry. I appreciate what has been revealed to them about both. Christmas is prophecy fulfilled! For their prophecies "came not in old time by the will of man; but holy men of God spake as they were moved by the Holy Ghost" (1 Peter 1:21). As Elder Mark E. Peterson observed, "Without the Restoration, the true meaning of Christ's birth would still be a mystery to the groping world."

So curl up with a cup of hot chocolate and let the following chapters guide you through the symbols of the season and the real story of Christmas, dove-tailed with insights from the restored gospel of Jesus Christ. Here's wishing you a very Merry Christmas and an even more prosperous New Year!

Notes
1. C. S. Lewis, *The Case for Christianity* (New York: Macmillan, 1968), 36, 45.

TWO

CHRIST'S BIRTH

The Centerpiece of Christmas

THE CENTERPIECE ON ANY TABLE naturally attracts our attention and whispers, "You are welcome here." But Christmas centerpieces seem to glow and hold our interest longer than most. They're colorful, bright, and hint at something wonderfully exciting. The holly, mistletoe, and pine boughs draped around candles, laced with ornaments and tied with ribbon, warm our spirits. They remind us of the ties that bind us all heart-to-heart. This is especially true during this festive time of year.

There is, however, one centerpiece that binds all the symbols of the season together. "Christ's birth," Elder Neal A. Maxwell reminded us, "is the centerpiece of Christmas."[1] Christ is, in so many ways, not only the centerpiece of Christmas, but the centerpiece of our lives, and more important, the centerpiece of the Father's plan for our exaltation. It is significant that His birth came in the meridian of time. It was the midpoint, not the beginning of His ministry, which includes both pre- and post-mortal missions. Similarly, His teachings ought to be the center of our lives. Nothing is more important in mortality than becoming like Jesus Christ—following His teachings, understanding His Atonement, appreciating His intercession for us, and trying to pattern our lives after His supreme example so that "when he shall appear we shall be like him" (Moroni 7:48).

The Savior is the center of everything that really matters in mortality and throughout all eternity. So at Christmastime, our weary world pauses to dust itself off and lift itself up for a few weeks, to recall His miraculous birth and to remember His marvelous life. President Ezra Taft Benson said, "No other single influence has had so great an impact on this earth as the life of Jesus Christ. We cannot conceive of our lives without His teachings. Without Him we would be lost in a mirage of beliefs and worships, born in fear and darkness where the sensual and materialistic hold sway."[2]

WHAT THINK YE OF CHRIST?

"What think ye of Christ? Whose son is he?" (Matthew 22:42). Jesus asked these questions to a group of Pharisees and Sadducees who sought to entrap Him. Now, almost two thousand years later, Jesus Christ has been an eternal inspiration to countless millions—the greatest and mightiest figure of all mankind. Almost two millennia have come and gone since the Savior walked the earth, and with each passing year, His dominion grows larger.[3] But each new generation, every individual needs to answer the same question, "What think *ye* of Christ?" One really can't be neutral where Christ is concerned. It's not enough to know Him as *the* Savior or as *a* Redeemer. Each of us needs to know Him as *our personal* Savior (see John 17:3). We must learn more about Him. He invites us to "come unto" Him and to "come follow" Him.

The scriptures we possess—the iron rod that leads to the tree of life "whose fruit is desirable to make one happy" (1 Nephi 8:19)—lead us to Christ and help us know Him. Coupled with the living testimony of those who have been called to preside in this dispensation, the scriptures are, without question, the primary source of our understanding of His doctrines and of His divine character. We are very blessed to have the records we do. We don't even have a complete canon of that first Christmas—"And there are many other things which Jesus did, the which, if they should be written every one, I suppose that even the world itself could not contain the books that should be written" (John 21:25)—but we do have enough to learn of Him, to have faith in Him, to love and appreciate Him, to come unto Him, and to receive the blessings He alone can give.

But, unfortunately, "just as there was no room for Christ in the inn," Elder Maxwell observed, "even so, there is no room for Christ in the inn-tellect of many in today's world."[4] How would we regard and treat this man today with his "strange" and "impractical" doctrines of human behavior? Do we believe and follow any more than the people of His day believed and followed? Are we any more prepared for the Second Coming of Christ than they were for His first?

Anciently, Christ was not acknowledged, even by those who knew the prophecies. As President Gordon B. Hinckley noted, "He was not accepted as the Savior, the Redeemer, the promised Messiah. A handful believed Him, but the multitude scorned Him, He who had come to save them from their sins and bring to them peace and love and everlasting life."[5]

FAITH IN CHRIST—THE FIRST PRINCIPLE

We can never dilute the Savior's declarations about Himself or His divinity. Those who are baptized have covenanted to stand "as witnesses of God at all times [including Christmastime] and in all things, and in all places" (Mosiah 18:9). Those who stand up for Christ in this life will be privileged to walk with Him in the next (compare Daniel 3:16–20, 24–25). None are denied this opportunity. None are exempt. All have an open invitation (2 Nephi 9:21; 26:33; 3 Nephi 17:17–25).

In order to stand as sure witnesses for the Savior, we have to develop greater faith in Him, His life, and His mission. Faith in the Lord Jesus Christ is the first principle of the restored gospel, not the second (see Articles of Faith 1:4). In order for any "rational and intelligent" human being to exercise faith in God—for that faith to become a force for good in their lives—and to enable their faith to anchor their souls "unto life and salvation," the Prophet Joseph Smith taught that three things are necessary:

"First, the idea that [God] actually exists.

"Secondly, a correct idea of his character, perfections, and attributes.

"Thirdly, an actual knowledge that the course of life which he is pursuing is according to [God's] will."[6]

The Prophet Joseph was right—we cannot have adequate faith in a Christ we do not adequately know, "who is a stranger . . . far from the thoughts and intents of our hearts" (Mosiah 5:13).[7] As President Howard W. Hunter observed, "The real Christmas comes to him who has taken Christ into his life as a moving, dynamic, vitalizing source."[8] And this understanding comes through the words recorded in the scriptures, through the power of human testimony, and from the declarations of prophets who know the

Lord. As the Apostle Paul declared, "Faith cometh by hearing . . . the word of God" (Romans 10:17).

Faith in God is more than a one-time confession that we believe in Christ. It is more than a positive mental attitude about life—more than a feeling that we can succeed at whatever we set out to do. It is a principle of power and salvation by which we can develop a spiritual union with the Lord and qualify to return where He reigns. It is faith in Him, that He desires to and will help us in time of need. This kind of faith begins with a comprehension of how utterly and absolutely dependent we are on God—to "always retain in remembrance the greatness of God"—and sense our own nothingness, that without Him, we truly are "less than the dust of the earth" (see Mosiah 2:25, 3:11; Helaman 12:7–25). We need His help. But it is not always easy to believe that He can, or will, help us. Moroni reminded us, "Faith is things which are hoped for and not seen" (Ether 12:6). We believe in Christ, but to have faith in Him is to believe Him, to believe that He can lift us, change us, perfect us (so that we have no defects, no character flaws), stablish us (so that we won't be shaken by winds of doubt), strengthen us (so that we will not weaken before temptation), help us become rooted and built up in Him (so that we establish our lives and philosophies on His solid foundation), and settle us (so that we will no longer take counsel from fear) (see 1 Peter 5:10; Colossians 1:7; and Ephesians 3:17). Our Heavenly Father can make us "steadfast, immovable, always abounding in good works . . . so that the Lord may seal us his" (Mosiah 5:15), but we need to believe it! Faith in Christ is to no longer fear, to no longer dwell on our failings, to no longer doubt our righteous desires.

The blessings flowing from such resolute faith in Christ keep us from being "moved away from the hope of the gospel" (Colossians 1:23). And that hope is the assurance of eternal life. "Wherefore, whoso believeth in God might with surety hope for [expect] a better world, yea, even a place at the right hand of God, which hope cometh of faith, maketh an anchor to the souls of men, which would make them sure and steadfast, always abounding in good works, being led to glorify God" (Ether 12:4).

What would Christmas be like if each of us could lay hold on these gifts because of our faith and hope in Christ!

COMING TO KNOW CHRIST

Christmas is the perfect time to experience the life-changing realization that Alma and his people came to: "And now it came to pass that all this was done in Mormon, yea, by the waters of Mormon, in the forest that was near the waters of Mormon; yea, the place of Mormon, the waters of Mormon, the forest of Mormon, how beautiful are they to the eyes of them who there came to the knowledge of their Redeemer; yea, and how blessed are they, for they shall sing to his praise forever (Mosiah 18:30). Whenever, and wherever, we come to know Christ, that time and that place will be sacred to us forever. Why not make Christmas that kind of time in our lives, that kind of experience?

The Christmas season is a perfect time to enlarge our understandings of the greatest of all gifts, the gift of Jesus, the Savior of mankind. Out of gratitude we can become a little kinder, a little more thoughtful of others, a little more generous, more helpful, as one Milwaukee teenager named Frank Daily demonstrated. A few years ago he took off his shoes and gave them to a needy woman who got on a bus in her stocking feet to escape the frigid streets.[9] "I felt sorry for her," Frank said after he handed the woman his shoes. "It was very cold out and she looked really worn. I figured we'll probably always have enough money to get shoes. She'll probably never have enough."

The bus driver, John Williams, who witnessed the moment, said the pregnant woman, about thirty-five years of age, got on the bus wearing a tattered coat and ripped socks with no shoes. He guessed it was about ten degrees outside and said the woman was going downtown, headed in the opposite direction, but she got on his bus anyway because she was cold.

The woman told Williams she had enough money to buy shoes for her eight children but not for herself. They were still talking when Frank Daily got up to leave. "That kid walked up with his shoes in his hand and just handed them to the woman," Williams said. "He was barefooted. Imagine giving your shoes to someone else on a day like that. He just looked at her and said 'Here, lady, you need these more than me.' Tears came to my eyes." The woman also started crying.

"She was touched. She'll never forget Frank," he said. "I just get the chills every time I think about it." When asked why he would do such an unselfish thing, Daily modestly replied, "The deed was nothing. After all, it's Christmas."

So often mortality is like a night in a second-class hotel.[10] But it's meeting and knowing people (even better, being) like Frank Daily that makes this second-estate a real first-class experience. The "peaceable followers of Christ" (Moroni 7:3) are more interested in the souls of others than in the kinds of soles they wear.

Elder Bruce R. McConkie shared an experience from his family in which his grandmother came to know the verity of King Benjamin's injunction that "when ye are in the service of your fellow beings, ye are only in the service of your God" (Mosiah 2:17). Elder McConkie said:

> For a text I shall read to you a brief statement from the journal of my father in which he speaks of his mother and of my grandmother. My grandmother, Emma Sommerville McConkie, was a ward Relief Society president in Moab, Utah, many years ago. At the time of this experience, she was a widow.
>
> My father writes this: "Mother was president of the Moab Relief Society. [Mr. __, a man who opposed the Church] had married a Mormon girl. They had several children; now they had a new baby. They were very poor and Mother was going day by day to care for the child and to take them baskets of food, etc. Mother herself was ill, and more than once was hardly able to get home after doing the work at the[ir] home.
>
> One day she returned home especially tired and weary. She slept in her chair. She dreamed she was bathing a baby which she discovered was the Christ Child. She thought, Oh, what a great honor to thus serve the very Christ! As she held the baby in her lap, she was all but overcome. She thought, who else has actually held the Christ Child? Unspeakable joy filled her whole being. She was aflame with the glory of the Lord. It seemed that the very marrow in her bones would melt. Her joy was so great it awakened her. As she woke, these words were spoken to her, "'Inasmuch as ye have done it unto one of the least of these my brethren, ye have done it unto me."[11]

THERE IS NO OTHER WAY

The Creator of this world has given us everything we have, everything we need. And then He gave us His life. We are forever in his debt (Mosiah 2:23). That's why every mile trod by our pioneer ancestors, every league sailed by those who gave up homes and families for the gospel's call, every log rolled into place in each new settlement, every brick and stone set with mortar, every building and temple erected, every article written, every magazine and manual published, every testimony borne in sacrament meetings, have all been done with the single, focused purpose to bear witness that Jesus is the Savior, our Redeemer—to "teach and invite all to come unto Christ" (D&C 20:59) "and be perfected in him" (Moroni

10:32). We have been commanded to do this precisely because there is no other way, no other plan, and no other person who can make eternal life a reality for us (Acts 4:12). There was no backup plan, no second Messiah waiting in the wings to come onstage (see 2 Nephi 25:20). There is no salvation in false doctrine. "Salvation can come unto the children of men, only in and through the name of Christ, the Lord Omnipotent" (Mosiah 3:17; 2 Nephi 25:20).

When Christ came into the world, He also came *unto* the world. He was sent here to each of us. His whole "work and glory" is to bring to pass our eternal life and immortality (Moses 1:39). In Gethsemane and on Calvary, He worked out the infinite and eternal Atonement. It was the greatest single act of love in recorded history. Then followed His death and miraculous resurrection. "I came into the world to do the will of my Father, because my Father sent me. And my Father sent me that I might be lifted up upon the cross" (3 Nephi 27:13–14). And so He was. Thus He became our Redeemer, redeeming all of us from physical death, and redeeming those of us from spiritual death who will obey the laws and ordinances of His gospel. "To this end was I born," the Savior fearlessly declared to Pilate, "for this cause came I into the world" (John 18:37).

Father Lehi tenderly witnessed to his son, Jacob, this same solemn truth: "Wherefore, redemption cometh in and through the Holy Messiah. . . . Behold he offereth himself a sacrifice for sin, to answer the ends of the law, unto all those who have a broken heart and a contrite spirit. . . . Wherefore, how great the importance to make these things known unto the inhabitants of the earth, that they may know that there is no flesh that can dwell in the presence of God, save it be through the merits, and mercy, and grace of the Holy Messiah . . . and they that believe in him shall be saved" (2 Nephi 2:6–9).

Notes

1. Neal A. Maxwell, unpublished Christmas address delivered in the Salt Lake Monument Park Stake, Dec. 1986, transcript in possession of author.

2. Ezra Taft Benson, in Conference Report, Apr. 1971, 19.

3. Gordon B. Hinckley, quoted in "He Came As Babe in Manger, Not in Glory," *LDS Church News*, Dec. 7, 1991, 4.

4. Neal A. Maxwell, unpublished address delivered in the Salt Lake Monument Park Stake, Dec. 1986.

5. Gordon B. Hinckley, "He Came As Babe," 3.

6. *Lectures on Faith*, Lecture 3:2–5, comp. N. B. Lundwall (Salt Lake City: Bookcraft), 33.

7. See Neal A. Maxwell, in Conference Report, Apr. 1986, 45.

8. Howard W. Hunter, "The Real Christmas," *BYU Speeches of the Year*, 1972–73 (Provo, Utah: Brigham Young University Press, 1973), 68.

9. See "Teen Bares Feet to Shoe Woman," *Deseret News*, Salt Lake City, Utah, Dec. 10, 1984.

10. Saint Teresa of Avila deserves credit for the analogy, as quoted by Malcolm Muggeridge, "The Great Liberal bath Wish," *Imprimis*, May 1979 (Hillsdale College: Michigan); also cited in Neal A. Maxwell, *All These Things Shall Give Thee Experience* (Salt Lake City: Deseret Book, 1979), 50.

11. Bruce R. McConkie, *Sermons and Writings of Bruce R. McConkie* (Salt Lake City: Bookcraft, 1998), 388.

THREE

Symbolism vs. Commercialism

I N A N A G E O F S O P H I S T I C A T I O N and commercialism, the world is experiencing a greater need for the power and peace of the gospel of Jesus Christ. Many long for better days. We hunger and thirst after righteousness, and His promise to us is that we will be "filled" (3 Nephi 12:6). "Come unto me," the Savior beckoned, "and I will give you rest" (Matthew 11:28). He asked us, "What think ye of Christ?" (Matthew 22:42). And then He extended numerous invitations for us to get to know Him: Learn of Me (Matthew 11:29); Come Follow Me (Luke 18:22); Come unto Christ and Be Perfected in Him (Moroni 10:32); I Am the Light (3 Nephi 18:27); Even as I Am (3 Nephi 27:27); I Am the Way, the Truth, the Life (John 14:6); If Ye Love Me, Keep My Commandments (John 14:15). He testifies that "I have set an Example for you" (3 Nephi 18:16) and his prophets invite us to "come unto Christ and be perfected in him" (Moroni 10:32).

We have been graciously invited to "feast," not "nibble" at the table of the Lord (2 Nephi 31:20 and 32:3). And it's not just Gerber Gospel that we're being offered—it's the fulness of all dispensations, restored in these latter days. "Come . . . every one that thirsteth, come ye to the waters . . . Come unto the Holy One of Israel, and feast on that which perisheth not, neither can be corrupted, and let your soul delight in fatness" (2 Nephi 9:50–51).

When you stop to contemplate all of the blessings we have been given—including life, an opportunity to prove ourselves; this wonderful planet on which we live (which one day will become a celestial orb, the celestial kingdom for us); the fulness of the restored gospel; the privilege of serving each other; the blessing of having living prophets, seers, and revelators; the Atonement that makes it possible to overcome sin, error and weakness; and the resurrection and possibility of eternal life in the presence of our Father—the thought of how truly marvelous the Messiah is can be overwhelming.

We wish we could have been there with Him in Jerusalem, to thank Him, to follow Him. And we can! Not physically, of course, but spiritually we can go to Bethlehem and sit with shepherds who heard angelic choirs. We can watch the faithfulness of those in ancient America the night before He was born. We can travel with the wise men who came seeking the infant-king. We can ponder with Mary the incredible experiences she kept in her heart—because we have the scriptures! Reading scriptures is like experiencing armchair history. But we must do more than idly observe. Like the wise men, we need to search for Christ by reading, pondering, praying, and then doing something about it. And unlike the innkeeper, we need to let Him in—"Where meek souls will receive Him still, the dear Christ enters in."[1] Or as John the Baptist declared, we must "prepare ye the way of the Lord, make his paths straight"—we must clear the way in our lives for Him and His teachings to reach us (Matthew 3:3).

There are so many lessons to be learned from the sacred account of Christ's birth. One of the most exciting and rewarding things about going to Bethlehem with Joseph and Mary each year in the scriptures is the discovery of new thoughts and greater insights into the life of Christ, which lead ultimately to greater thoughts and insights about our own lives and how to live them more abundantly. "I am come that they might have life, and that they might have it more abundantly," the Savior taught (see John 10:10). As President David O. McKay observed, "What you sincerely in your heart think of Christ . . . will determine what you are [and] will largely determine what your acts will be."[2] "No man can sincerely resolve to apply to his daily life the teachings of Jesus of Nazareth without sensing a change in his own nature. The phrase 'born again' has a deeper significance than many people attach to it. This changed feeling may be indescribable, but it is real. Happy is the person who has truly sensed the uplifting, transforming power that comes from this nearness to the Savior, this kinship to the Living Christ."[3]

President Benson has also described how the Lord can change us and lift us triumphantly above the problems we face in the world: "The Lord works from the inside out. The world works from the outside in. The world would take people out of the slums. Christ takes the slums out of people, and then they take themselves out of the slums. The world would mold men by changing their environment. Christ changes men, who then change their environment. The world would shape human behavior, but Christ can change human nature."[4]

CHILDISH ILLUSIONS OR ILLUMINATIONS?

The marvelous thing about Christmas is that it offers each individual another opportunity to change. All of us have had the experience of being at that awkward age—still wanting to feel the thrill of Christmas but too old to enjoy what maturity has forced us to leave behind. Do you remember the excitement of lying awake, unable to sleep, and the fun of running down early to see what Santa brought? We long to cling to that Christmas feeling we once had, yet we know that it was all a childish fantasy, so we quickly conclude that "Christmas is for kids."

Speaking to students at Brigham Young University about the importance of keeping Christmas (even as we get older), Elder Boyd K. Packer made an observation with a choice promise:

> There is a special spirit, an actual spirit that envelops the earth at this time. However much it may not differ from the spirit that is available at any time of the year, at this time of the year it seems to be prevalent and present in an intensity not known at other times of the year. It becomes so forceful as to have real, tangible, noticeable, effect on people who otherwise seem to avoid, or at least disregard, the spirit of the Lord. . . . If you would understand what you get in exchange for giving up the childish illusion concerning Christmas, you could look forward to the greatest of all discoveries. If you could just know that at your age you can find and can have that 'little kid' feeling again about Christmas. If you understand Christmas at all, you will find that in exchange for Christmas past comes the most supernal of gifts.[5]

When we were children we understood and thought as children, but when we're older we put away childish things. Paul's words to the Corinthians reflect the spiritual maturity we all are striving for: "For we know in part, and we prophesy in part. But when that which is perfect is come, then that which is in part shall be done away. When I was a child, I spake like a child, I thought as a child: but when I became a man, I put away childish things" (1 Corinthians 13:11). "Behold, ye are little children and ye cannot bear all things now; ye must grow in grace and in the knowledge of the truth" (D&C 50:40). As we grow in the "knowledge of the truth" we become less fettered in fables. To grow in "grace" we need to understand, accept, and apply the gift of the Atonement in our lives. The greatest of all discoveries come to those who leave the illusions of Christmas behind and come to understand the True Centerpiece of what Christmas is really all about.

The train leaving Toyland moves down the tracks of life slowly, line upon line, allowing us to "grow" out of a lot of things (see D&C 93:20; 98:12). But somehow with Christmas it's different. The Christmas train seems to move along at a reasonable pace, until suddenly one day the whole thing derails! Try as we may, we can never go back. "Toyland, Toyland, little girl and boy land, While we dwelled within it we were ever happy then. Childhood joyland, mystic, merry joyland. Once you've passed its portals you may ne'er return again."

As we put away the childish things of Christmas, we tend to despise what we leave behind. We may feel a sense of loss, disillusionment, perhaps even betrayal. "Can you remember when you knew just a little bit less about Christmas than you do now?" asked Elder Packer. "Do you remember when you still believed? If there is a feeling of disappointment in you at Christmastime, and if you suffer a longing for times as they were, it means you never really discovered Christmas at all—only the child's manifestation of it. Once you have lost your childhood, you have somehow lost that manifestation of it."[6]

Little wonder that so many adults feel an emptiness when stores start putting up Christmas displays. The gnawing sense of disillusion soon swells to a crescendo of complete apathy. "Bah, humbug," the Scrooge in us mutters. And every year a few misguided men, like old Ebenezer himself, begin to think of Christmas, and everything with it, as little more than "a poor excuse to pick a man's pocket once a year!"

A few years ago a *Church News* editorial described three levels of Christmas.[7] The first was called the "Santa Claus level." It is the level of Christmas trees, food, fun, decorations, colorful packages, shopping and socials in warm open houses, excited children, and exhausted but loving parents; the level at which we "eat too much and spend too much and do too much—and enjoy every minute of it." But soon the tree dries out and the needles fall. The toys break, the dieting begins, and we notice that the lonely and hungry are still with us.

A higher and more fulfilling level of Christmas could be called the "Silent Night level." It is the enjoyment of all beautiful Christmas carols, the magnificent Nativity, the shepherds in the hills near Bethlehem, angels with their glad tidings, the new star, and wise men travelling from afar in search of the Holy One. But even this level will not long satisfy the desperate needs of a fallen world. Those who keep Christ in the manger will never find the mature Savior, and will, in the end, still be disappointed and empty.

For Christmas to meet all the expectations of both child and adult, for Christmas to last all year long and grow in beauty and spirit, it must have the power to change lives. And that only happens on the third level, the "level of the Resurrected Lord," the level of the adult Christ. It is here we find lasting joy, lasting hope, and lasting peace. This level teaches us of charity, forgiveness, and love for the unlovable, forgiveness for enemies. This is the adult Christ who gave us a perfect example and asked us to follow Him. "Accepting that invitation is the way—the only way—to celebrate Christmas all year and all life long."[8]

THROUGH THE EYES OF A CHILD

As we give up childish things, we need to fill the void with greater childlike faith if we want to enjoy Christmas as much as we used to. Second birth comes when we overcome self and see through the eyes we had as children. Not that we become children again, but that we are more childlike. "Whosoever shall not receive the kingdom of God as a little child," the Savior taught, "shall not enter therein" (Mark 10:15). Elder Packer noted, "We have every encouragement to adopt the attitude, 'seeing is believing.' The remarkable thing is that if you hold that spirit, you do not have the hope or the chance of ever finding Christmas as it ought to be, because, you see, it is just the other way around, 'believing is seeing.' "[9]

The kingdom of God, like the true spirit of Christmas, is reserved only for those who see through the eyes of a child—who look to God with childlike faith. New and exciting things come more clearly into focus, things we were not previously able to notice because of the childish eyes through which we saw.

OPENING THE EYES OF OUR UNDERSTANDING

Reading the scriptures at Christmastime helps to wash away the worldly things that tend to dim our spiritual vision so that, like Enoch, for example, we can see more clearly "and behold things which were not visible to the natural eye" (Moses 6:35–36). To help Enoch better appreciate this, the Lord instructed him to cover his eyes with mud, symbolic of the things of the earth, and to then wash them clean. When the "world" was washed away, Enoch could see through the eyes of the Spirit. Similarly, we can learn to improve our spiritual vision at Christmas. However, it takes effort. Casual or occasional reading of the scriptures during the holidays may not be enough to see beyond the holiday tinsel and trappings. The Prophet Joseph Smith taught that the things of God are of such deep import that only time and experience and careful ponderous and solemn thought can find them out.[10]

One of the most rewarding scripture-study experiences is to read the Joseph Smith Translation. The JST is the best Bible on the earth. Wherever possible, I have used the inspired changes from the JST that were revealed to the Prophet Joseph Smith. Those changes offer new light and new understanding to this age-old story.

The symbols of Christmas are merely external manifestations of a far deeper and spiritual truths. Indeed, they are beautiful and gratifying expressions of His character or of the larger, more complete eternal purposes and promises of His plan. Each symbol can teach us something about Christ's divine nature. To look beyond the symbols and discover the sublime, real meaning behind them is to experience the greatest of all holiday discoveries. And like true symbols, greater spiritual maturity brings greater insight. Whether you like these symbols or not, consider the mighty realities for which they stand!

SYMBOLISM OVER SUBSTANCE

Children hear so much about the Tooth Fairy, Easter Bunny, Santa Claus, and Jesus that they could begin to think of them all in the same way—as fairy tales, myths, legends, and lores. The trappings of Christmas cluttered around the Centerpiece can both add to the spirit of what Christmas is as well as detract from it. Thus the annual debate will be renewed about whether Christmas has become too commercialized. The potential for crisis and conflict between spiritual and commercial is never greater, the demand for spiritual insight never more compelling than during the Christmas rush when gold, frankincense, and myrrh go on sale. Like all symbols, if one becomes too preoccupied with the symbol itself, forgetting to look beyond it and see the "mighty realities for which the symbol stands,"[11] he will surely feel some sense of loss or disappointment. Elder John A. Widtsoe commented about the strained relationship between symbolism and Christmas: "There are men who object to Santa Claus, because he does not exist! Such men need spectacles to see that Santa Claus is a symbol; a symbol of the love and joy of Christmas and the Christmas spirit. In the land of my birth there was no Santa Claus, but a little goat was shoved into the room, carrying with it a basket of Christmas toys and gifts. The goat of itself counted for nothing; but the Christmas spirit, which it symbolized, counted for a tremendous lot."[12]

Certain questions about the symbols of Christmas need to be given careful consideration and settled in our hearts so that we can enjoy the holiday more.

First, should the symbols be done away with entirely? There's little question that Santa and Rudolph can distract us from the things that really matter most, if we allow them to. They can be exploited to the point that the Light and Life of the world is trampled under the feet of shoppers rushing home with their treasures. Christmas is not who comes down the chimney, but who comes down from heaven. The prophet Nephi warned, "For the things which some men esteem to be of great worth, both to the body and soul, others set at naught [despise, reject, count for nothing] and trample under their feet. Yea, even the very God of Israel do men trample under their feet; I say, trample under their feet but I would speak in other words—they set him at naught, and hearken not to the voice of his counsels" (1 Nephi 19:7). Clearly, any attempt to have Christmas symbols without the substance could prove harmful "both to the body and soul" just as Nephi said. The efforts of some to entirely do away with the "mighty realities for which the symbols stand" and keep only the symbols of Christmas have some tremendous social, cultural, and religious implications. We cannot trivialize away what the symbols stand for if we expect the Bright and Morning Star (Christ) to arise in our hearts at Christmastime (see Revelation 2:28; 22:16; 1 Peter 1:19).

Second, by clinging to the symbols and fun of Christmas, do we run the risk of setting our hearts on temporal things? Remember that "temporal" means temporary. The ornaments are only on display in our homes a short time each year. They are not what's important. As with Christmas, so it is with life. The things of this world can never become the center of our heart's desire. "None of the presents under the tree, none of the plaques and certificates hanging on our walls are portable. Only our character goes with us, and it is the journey of journeys here in mortality to become like Him. His plea to us—speed up the process."[13] (See D&C 130:18–19). To take clues about who we are from the "temporary" gifts, awards, and achievements that come from others takes our focus away from our eternal identity as a child of God. That's who we are. That's who, eternally, we'll go on being. Presidents of clubs and organizations, most valuable player on the team, salesperson of the year, and every other "temporal" award bestowed upon us loses significance at death. But our character, our identity as a child of God and as brothers and sisters, lasts forever. As Elder Maxwell so pointedly reminded us, "One day all our temporary designations, locations, and vocations will shrink in their significance when bathed in the candlepower of Kolob's brighter and perfect day. . . . What finally matters, brothers and sisters, is what we have become. There will be no puffed vitae circulating in the next world. They stay here—in the files. What we will take with us—to the degree we have developed them—will be the cardinal qualities that Jesus has perfected; these are eternal and portable."[14]

Eternal blessings have been lost because people have settled their hearts on the fleeting things of the moment, worldly things, and the honors of men (see Genesis 25:29–34). Hence, many who were called fail to have their calling and election made sure. "And why are they not chosen? Because their hearts are set so much upon the things of this world, and they aspire to the honors of men" (D&C 121:34–35; Helaman 7:20–21). The challenge in this temporal world is to stay focused on eternal things. And distractions don't need to be sinful to be wrong. They only have to distract us long enough to do the damage: "Ye are cursed because of your riches, and also are your riches cursed because ye have set your hearts upon them, and have not hearkened unto the words of him who gave them unto you. Ye do not remember the Lord your God in the things which he hath blessed you, but ye do always remember your riches, not to thank the Lord your God for them; yea, your hearts are not drawn out unto the Lord, but they do swell with great pride, unto boasting, and unto great swelling, envyings, strifes, malice, persecutions, and murders, and all manner of iniquities" (Helaman 13:21–22).

Third, we might want to ask ourselves if we think we can successfully separate the symbols of Christmas from the Savior. An even greater question may be, would you really want to? We cannot share the symbols under, around, and on the Christmas tree, and then go away and celebrate the true meaning of Christmas as if the two have nothing in common. The greatest understanding of Christmas cannot be fulfilled if we hastily and surreptitiously dismiss the litany of symbols surrounding us, especially without remembering why they were given. Our greatest difficulty, really, is not the symbols, but our failure to communicate what they represent.

Besides, Christmas symbols are everywhere. We'll never be able to avoid seeing them. Trying to is like saying, "Okay, the world has polluted the air, but I don't have to breathe it!" It just doesn't work because the popular lore will continue to multiply with more stories about elves and reindeer. No matter how Santa's used or abused, he's with us forever. "To lift a line from Pogo," one modern writer observed, "Sir, I have seen Santa Claus. He is us."[15]

Children growing up in today's world should know and at some point need to learn, however, that not all of the voices calling to them, not all of the "causes" asking for their participation may be good to be involved with. Christmas affords us the perfect opportunity to learn how to distinguish between the important and the trivial. Moroni taught us how to judge: Everything which "inviteth to do good *and* persuade to believe in Christ . . . is of God" (Moroni 7:16–17; emphasis added). Too often we forget the second phrase in that warning, "*and* persuade to believe in Christ." Something may appear to be a good thing, socially acceptable, and politically correct, but if, in the end, it leads us away from Christ, it will not be good for us.

Nevertheless, we can successfully mix the two (the symbols of Christmas and the Savior) and enjoy both, without hastily and guiltily retreating into separate worlds each Christmas season—if we allow one to bear witness of the other. Looking at a symbol means looking "beyond" it to understand that these figures are merely tokens of what Christmas is all about—types of a greater reality, of something that demands special sanctity—the Savior. Each Christmas custom and every Christmas symbol helps us remember, and appreciate more, some greater truth about Christ. We can teach our children to distinguish between the symbol and the substance so that they can see that "all things have their likeness, and all things are created and made to bear record of me" precisely as the Savior testified to Moses (Moses 6:63).

The real question at Christmastime is, do we honor God as much as we do men, fairy tales, and folklore? The difference in enjoying the more secular festivities and the more important spiritual celebrations is one of understanding their proper place and role. If Shakespeare or Santa were to come into the room, for example, we would all stand up. If Jesus Christ came into the room, we would all kneel down. One of my favorite Christmas ornaments depicts Santa Claus kneeling before the Christ child lying in a crèche. We need to remember Him and appreciate what He did. Symbols help us do that. Without His help we would have all remained unclean and unresurrected spirits throughout all eternity (2 Nephi 9:6–10). We would have become "devils, angels to a devil, to be shut out from the presence of our God . . . to remain with the father of lies, in misery, like unto himself" (2 Nephi 9:9). Oh how great the wisdom and the love of Christ for us, who prepared the way for us to escape an otherwise certain and awful fate!

Symbols can't be swept under the rug for another important reason. Even the real story of Christmas, found in the scriptures, is rich in symbolism and figurative expression. The ability to look at the world through childlike eyes and see greater beauty and purpose is a gift that can be transferred to our personal study of the prophets' writings. One thing that makes the story come alive when we read it is to have the Spirit unveil or reveal hidden meanings about those many symbols.

"THIS DO IN REMEMBRANCE OF ME"

In addition to the symbols and scriptures, we have also been given other important types and representations of Christ—ordinances and sacred ceremonies. The ancient Passover, for example, helped the children of Israel "look forward" to and anticipate the Atonement, just as the sacrament helps Latter-day Saints to "look back" and remember what He did. When the Savior blessed the sacrament at the Passover meal, He said, "This do in remembrance of me" (Luke 22:19). The sacrament we take each week is a type of Christ. The bread reminds us that His torn body would resurrect, and the water reminds us that His blood was shed for us. The eternal sacrifice He paid in the Garden of Gethsemane and on the cross at Calvary fully satisfied the demands of justice so we could be cleansed of our sins and be resurrected from death. Thus, the emblems of the sacrament help us remember the greatness of His wisdom and love.

Even so, the emblems of Christmas can open our eyes to an even greater understanding and appreciation of Christ.

It's interesting that only Luke's Gospel used the word *remembrance* in connection with the sacrament. In Joseph Smith's inspired revision of the New Testament, he changed both Matthew and Mark's accounts to include the word *remember*. Luke's account, which already used *remember*, was not changed by the Prophet.[16] Both of our modern sacrament prayers use the words *remember* and *remembrance*, promising that if we do it will be our privilege to "always have his spirit to be with us" (D&C 20:77, 79). "Remember, remember," Helaman taught his sons, "that it is upon the rock of our Redeemer, who is Christ, the Son of God, that ye must build your foundation . . . a sure foundation, a foundation whereon if men build they cannot fall" (Helaman 5:12). Similarly, if we build the symbols of Christmas on Christ, we won't fail to experience the real spirit of Christmas. President Spencer W. Kimball said that the word *remember* might just be one of the most important words in our language: "When you look in the dictionary for the most important word, do you know what it is? It could be 'remember.' Because all of you have made covenants—you know what to do and how to do it—our greatest need is to remember. That is why everyone goes to sacrament meeting every Sabbath day—to take the sacrament and listen to the priests pray that they '. . . may always remember him and keep his commandment which he has given them; . . . ' Nobody should ever forget to go to sacrament meeting. 'Remember' is the word. 'Remember' is the program."[17]

All of our favorite Christmas symbols have deeper meanings associated with them. Whether you enjoy these Christmas customs and symbols of the Savior during this special season or not, at least ponder the "mighty realities" for which they stand.

UNWRAP THE GREATEST OF ALL GIFTS THIS CHRISTMAS

We can make the journey to Bethlehem with Mary and Joseph in spirit. The time we spend visiting the Christ child by reading the scriptures can be a very rich and meaningful experience, or it can be commonplace and have little effect. "With careful preparation and the help of the Spirit, you can reread the age-old story with new life, new meaning, and new power."[18] This book is dedicated to helping you have that experience. Beginning with the next chapter, you'll be able to read the real story of

Christmas, studying the scriptures sequentially but arranged in a chrono-logical order, and using the Joseph Smith Translation,[19] so you can experience the Nativity just as it unfolded anciently.

As you do, may your family be blessed with the knowledge and wisdom and peace that can only come as we seek after the Savior. May you rediscover Him during this holiday season when His Spirit manifests itself so abundantly everywhere. This wonderful spirit of Christmas is not something that can be put into a jar or tied with ribbons and tags. It is something so precious no money can buy it, so rare no store in the world can sell it, so unique everyone can enjoy it. "The Christmas spirit is the Spirit of Christ that makes our hearts glow in brotherly love and friendship and prompts us to kind deeds of service," the First Presidency (Ezra Taft Benson, Gordon B. Hinckley, Thomas S. Monson) wrote: "The Christmas season offers an opportunity to renew our quest for the true Spirit of Christ and to focus our attention not only on His birth, but also on the teachings of His mortal ministry, the incredible sacrifice made for us all through His suffering and death, and His glorious resurrection and the accompanying assurance of everlasting life to all humankind."[20]

Like the Second Coming, Christmas can be both great and dreadful, depending on our preparation. May we preserve the spirit of this season all year round, and may we be better prepared to focus on the things that really matter most. Christ truly is, and ought to be, the Centerpiece of this special season.

Notes

1. "O Little Town of Bethlehem," *Hymns*, no. 208.
2. David O. McKay, in Conference Report, Apr. 1951, 93.
3. David O. McKay, in Conference Report, Apr. 1962, 7.
4. Ezra Taft Benson, in Conference Report, Oct. 1985, 5.
5. Boyd K. Packer, "Keeping Christmas," *BYU Speeches of the Year*, Dec. 19, 1962, 2, 5.
6. Boyd K. Packer, "Keeping Christmas," 3.
7. See "Three Levels of Christmas," *LDS Church News*, Dec. 15, 1985, 16.
8. Ibid.
9. Boyd K. Packer, "Keeping Christmas," 5.
10. Joseph Smith, *Teachings of the Prophet Joseph Smith*, sel. Joseph Fielding Smith (Salt Lake City: Deseret Book, 1976), 137.

11. Paraphrase of Elder John A. Widtsoe's quote about temple symbols in "Temple Worship," *Utah Genealogical and Historical Magazine*, 12 (Apr. 1921): 62.

12. Ibid.

13. Neal A. Maxwell, in an unpublished Christmas address to LDSSA students in Symphony Hall, Salt Lake City, Utah, Dec. 1991.

14. Neal A. Maxwell, "Out of the Best Faculty," *BYU Magazine*, 48 (Feb. 1994): 33, 48.

15. Jerry Johnston, "Santa: Ages of Goodness," *Deseret News*, Dec. 10, 1986, C-1.

16. I am indebted to Gerald N. Lund for this insight.

17. Spencer W. Kimball, "Circles of Exaltation," 8, address given to Church Education System employees, June 28, 1968.

18. *The Growing Edge*, Church Educational System newsletter, vol. 14 (Dec. 1981).

19. Two reasons for wanting to use the JST come from what the Lord Himself said about it. First, in a revelation to Moses, that the JST would restore the words written originally by the prophets: "And in a day when the children of men shall esteem my words as naught and take many of them from the book which thou [Moses] shalt write, behold, I will raise up another like unto thee [the Prophet Joseph]; and they shall be had again among as many as shall believe" (Moses 1:41). Second, in calling Sidney Rigdon to serve as a scribe for the Prophet Joseph, the Lord said the work of the JST would restore the scriptures "even as they are" in His own heart: "And a commandment I give unto thee—that thou shalt write for him; and the scriptures shall be given, even as they are in mine own bosom, to the salvation of mine own elect" (D&C 35:20).

20. Ezra Taft Benson, Gordon B. Hinckley, and Thomas S. Monson, First Presidency Christmas Message, *LDS Church News*, Dec. 21, 1986, 1.

FOUR

FAITHFUL WITNESSES

Whom I Have Chosen

S INCE CHRIST'S BIRTH IS THE Centerpiece of Christmas, it should not surprise us that Christ has been the center of all the prophets' writings from the beginning of time. "The Law and the prophets testify of me; yea, and all the prophets who have written, even until John [the Baptist] have foretold of these days" (JST, Luke 16:7). Although there was much diversity of opinion about when and how Jesus would come to earth, the certainty of His birth was fundamentally established in the beliefs and hopes of the Hebrew nation. Because of the writings of Israel's prophets, they knew more about His birth than any other people. "Every prophet," President Benson affirmed, "from the days of Adam knew of that first Christmas and testified of the divine ministry of the mortal Messiah."[1] "Yea, and even all the prophets who have prophesied ever since the world began—have they not spoken more or less concerning these things? Have they not said that God himself should come down among the children of men, and take upon him the form of man, and go forth in mighty power upon the face of the earth?" (Mosiah 13:33–34).

We sometimes think of Old Testament prophets as old men. Many of them were young and in the prime of their lives, filled with energy and enthusiasm when they began their ministries. Young in body, but matured well beyond their years by the Spirit, their testimonies have been painstakingly preserved so that their witnesses of the Messiah's birth and mission might be had in later generations. It is not mere coincidence that the particular scriptures we have today survived the ravages of time. The scriptures are not just histories, but they are testimonies—personal witnesses from every previous dispensation. Because of the prophets' efforts—labors of love—we see how clearly the events of Jesus' birth, life, and death were foretold and foreshadowed, so that we would make no mistake. "For, for this intent have we witnessed these things, that they may know that we knew of his Christ, and we had a hope of his glory many hundred years before his coming; and not only we ourselves had a hope of his glory, but also all the holy prophets which were before us. Behold, they believed in Christ and worshipped the Father in his name" (Jacob 4:4–5).

And, as Nephi declared, they wrote so that we could come unto Him: "We talk of Christ, we rejoice in Christ, we preach of Christ, we prophesy of Christ, and we write according to our prophecies, *that our children may know to what source they may look for a remission of their sins*" (2 Nephi 25:26; emphasis added). The Book of Mormon uniquely declares that because the Father knew that Jesus would, in fact, accomplish the Atonement, He allowed the blessings of the Atonement to work in people's lives, even before it was accomplished (Mosiah 3:13). For four thousand years prior to Christ's birth, prophets testified of Him and people exercised faith in Him unto repentance (Mosiah 16:6; 2 Nephi 25:26; Jarom 1:11).

Their testimonies are sure, and chief among the great events they foresaw was the birth and ministry of the Messiah.

THE PROPHECY IN THE GARDEN OF EDEN (ABOUT 4000 BC)

Our first parents were the first on earth to hear prophecy and to themselves prophesy about the birth and mission of our Savior. In the Garden of Eden, when God was explaining the consequences of the Fall, He said to the serpent (Lucifer): "I will put enmity between thee and the woman, between thy seed [Satan's followers] and her seed [Jesus Christ]; and it [Hebrew, *he*] shall bruise [Hebrew, *crush* or *grind*] thy head, and thou shalt bruise his heel" (Genesis 3:15).

The promise to Adam and Eve was that the "seed of the woman" would crush Satan's power completely. Throughout human history, Jesus Christ was the only person ever born on this earth who was born of a mortal mother but not a mortal father—the "seed of the woman."

The head of the serpent is the vital part of its body. The crushing of the head compared to the bruising of a heel metaphorically demonstrates the strength of the Lord to completely overpower and subdue Satan. God was telling Adam and Eve that Satan had power to bruise Christ's heel by getting men to crucify Him, but the very act would result in the Atonement and Resurrection, which overcome death and hell, crushing all power Satan might otherwise have over any of the children of men. Jacob described the danger we were in, a danger very real to Adam and Eve who were balanced on the eternal edge of the war for men's souls!

> Wherefore, the first judgment which came upon man must needs have remained to an endless duration. And if so, this flesh must have laid down to rot and to crumble to its mother earth, to rise no more. O the wisdom of God, his mercy and grace! For behold, if the flesh should rise no more our spirits must become subject to that angel who fell from before the presence of the Eternal God, and became the devil, to rise no more. And our spirits must have become like unto him, and we become devils, angels to a devil, to be shut out from the presence of our God, and to remain with the father of lies, in misery, like unto himself; yea, to that being who beguiled our first parents. (2 Nephi 9:7–9)

Most of the world blames Adam and Eve for the fallen condition we live in today. The whole Christian world has a great deal of enmity for them! Instead, we owe Adam and Eve a debt of gratitude and thanks. Without their fall, none of us would be here (see 2 Nephi 2:22–23). As President Joseph Fielding Smith has said of our primal parents, "Adam did only what he had to do. He partook of that fruit for one good reason, and that was to open the door to bring you and me and everyone else into this world, for Adam and Eve could have remained in the Garden of Eden; they could have been there to this day, if Eve hadn't done something. "So the commentators made a great mistake when they put in the Bible at the top of [one of the pages] the statement 'Man's shameful fall.' "[2]

It's unfortunate that most of the Christian world does not have the records of the restoration, because the Joseph Smith Translation makes it clear that Adam and Eve were taught about the coming of Christ and of His sacrifice, and were forgiven for the Fall and for their transgression in the Garden of Eden (see Moses 6:53).

When they were taught about baptism by immersion, Adam asked why men must repent and be baptized in water. The Eternal Father described the importance of Christ's birth to Father Adam:

And the Lord said unto Adam: Behold I have forgiven thee thy transgression in the Garden of Eden. Hence came the saying abroad among the people, that the Son of God hath atoned for original guilt.

Wherefore teach it unto your children, that all men, everywhere, must repent, or they can in nowise inherit the kingdom of God, for no unclean thing can dwell there, or dwell in his presence; for, in the language of Adam, Man of Holiness is his name, and the name of his Only Begotten is the Son of Man, even Jesus Christ, a righteous Judge, who shall come in the meridian of time.

Therefore I give unto you a commandment, to teach these things freely unto your children, saying:

That by reason of transgression cometh the fall, which fall bringeth death, and inasmuch as ye were born into the world by water, and blood, and the spirit, which I have made, and so became of dust a living soul, even so ye must be born again into the kingdom of heaven, of water, and of the Spirit, and be cleansed by blood, even the blood of mine Only Begotten; that ye might be sanctified from all sin, and enjoy the words of eternal life in this world, and eternal life in the world to come, even immortal glory;

And now, behold, I say unto you: This is the plan of salvation unto all men, through the blood of mine Only Begotten, who shall come in the meridian of time. (Moses 6:53–54, 57–59, 62)

Adam and Eve rejoiced to learn these things:

And in that day Adam blessed God and was filled [with the Holy Ghost], and began to prophesy concerning all the families of the earth, saying: Blessed be the name of God, for because of my transgression my eyes are opened, and in this life I shall have joy, and again in the flesh I shall see God.

And Eve, his wife, heard all these things and was glad, saying: Were it not for our transgression we never should have had seed, and never should have known good and evil, and the joy of our redemption, and the eternal life which God giveth unto all the obedient.

And Adam and Eve blessed the name of God, and they made all things known unto their sons and their daughters. (Moses 5:10–12)

THE PROPHECY OF ENOCH (ABOUT 3300 BC)

There are only four verses in the Old Testament about Enoch. The Prophet Joseph Smith's inspired translation adds over eighteen times as much! Without the Joseph Smith Translation we wouldn't even know there was a city of Enoch, let alone that it will one day return and that we will meet its inhabitants (see Moses 7:62–64).[3] But because of the Restoration, we now have Enoch's testimony of Christ.

Enoch saw "the day of the coming of the Son of Man." He fully understood the Savior's first coming as a mortal as well as His Second Coming "to dwell on the earth in righteousness for the space of a thousand years" (See Moses 7:45–67). In vision, he witnessed the prophet Noah's mission, the building of the ark, and the flood. "He wept over his brethren [his contemporaries who would be drowned in the flood], and said unto the heavens: I will refuse to be comforted; but the Lord said unto Enoch: Lift up your heart, and be glad; and look" (Moses 7:44). Enoch then recorded this beautiful testimony, which Joseph Smith restored to our scriptures:

> *And it came to pass that Enoch looked; and from Noah, he beheld all the families of the earth; and he cried unto the Lord, saying: When shall the day of the Lord come? When shall the blood of the Righteous be shed, that all they that mourn may be sanctified and have eternal life?*
>
> *And the Lord said: It shall be in the meridian of time. . . .*
>
> *And behold, Enoch saw the day of the coming of the Son of Man, even in the flesh; and his soul rejoiced, saying: The Righteous is lifted up, and the Lamb is slain from the foundation of the world.* (Moses 7:45–47)

THE PROPHECY OF NOAH (ABOUT 2400 bc)

After the flood had abated, the Lord promised Noah that He would never again destroy the earth by covering it with water (Genesis 9:9–11). He used the rainbow as a token and sign of this covenant[4] (Genesis 9:12–13; JST Genesis 9:24–25). The Joseph Smith Translation enlarges the scope of this covenant to include the return of Enoch's Zion to the earth and the Lord's promise to come again to dwell on the earth in the latter days. Noah was promised that not only would the Savior redeem mankind, but that when Noah's posterity (us) "embrace the truth, and look upward" that the "heavens shall shake with gladness, and the earth shall tremble with joy; And the general assembly of the church of the first-born [celestial beings] shall come down out of heaven, and possess this earth" (JST, Genesis 9:22–23). At the Second Coming, Christ will return with ten thousands of celestial beings, fulfilling this promise (see 1 Thessalonians 4:16–17; D&C 76:102; 84:100; 88:96; and 101:31). The meek will then inherit this earth and enjoy personal association with their Savior during the thousand-year millennium (see 3 Nephi 12:5). If those of us living in the latter days will learn to embrace the principles of Zion, we will, at His glorious Second Coming, be embraced by

Him! (See Moses 7:62–64.) As Jacob described it, "The keeper of the gate is the Holy One of Israel; and he employeth no servant there; and there is none other way save it be by the gate; for he cannot be deceived, for the Lord God is his name" (2 Nephi 9:41).

How divinely appropriate it was that Noah, the very prophet who witnessed the destruction of all mankind, was allowed the privilege to return to the earth and announce to Mary, Joseph, and Zacharias that Christ would be born to redeem all mankind. The angel Gabriel who heralded this glorious announcement is Noah.[5] His prophecies of Christ's birth are discussed in ensuing chapters.

THE PROPHECY OF MAHONRI MORIANCUMER (THE BROTHER OF JARED) (ABOUT 2300 BC)

Reynolds Cahoon and his wife, Thirza Stiles, had the last of their seven children, a baby boy, while living in Kirtland, Ohio. Shortly afterward, the Prophet Joseph was passing by the Cahoon home. Reynolds called upon the Prophet to bless and name their baby. Joseph did so and in the process of the blessing gave the boy the name *Mahonri Moriancumer*. When Joseph had finished the blessing, he said, "The name I have given your son is the name of the brother of Jared; the Lord has just shown [or revealed] it to me."[6]

Mahonri Moriancumer had the experience of seeing the Lord and talking with Him face to face (see Ether 3). He not only saw the Lord, he saw the physical flesh and blood body the Savior would take upon Himself as a mortal. The Book of Mormon records his testimony:

> And the Lord said unto him: Because of thy faith thou hast seen that I shall take upon me flesh and blood; and never has man come before me with such exceeding faith as thou hast. . . .
>
> And the Lord said unto him: Believest thou the words which I shall speak?
>
> And he answered: Yea, Lord, I know that thou speakest the truth, for thou art a God of truth, and canst not lie.
>
> Behold, I am he who was prepared from the foundation of the world to redeem my people. Behold, I am Jesus Christ. I am the Father and the Son. In me shall all mankind have life, and that eternally, even they who shall believe on my name; and they shall become my sons and my daughters.
>
> Behold, this body, which ye now behold, is the body of my spirit; and man have I created after the body of my spirit; and even as I appear unto thee to be in the spirit will I appear unto my people in the flesh. (Ether 3:9, 11–14, 16)

THE PROPHECY OF MOSES (ABOUT 1490 BC)

Moses was called to free the children of Israel from Egypt and deliver them to the promised land. Their deliverance came in the spring and has been celebrated by the Passover seder ever since. Spring is a time of renewal. Although not always associated with Christmas, the symbols of the exodus from Egypt and the Passover bear witness of our freedom from sin and spiritual rebirth, made possible by the birth of the Savior during the springtime, as the following insights show.

The children of Israel were finally freed from the clutches of Pharaoh and Egyptian bondage because of the death of all the firstborn (see Exodus 11:4–6). To help Israel remember the night the angel of death "passed over" Egypt and to point their minds forward to the time when Christ would be born and offer Himself as a sacrifice, the Lord instituted the Passover meal. Every aspect of the ceremony symbolized freedom and deliverance from bondage and sin through the Atonement of Christ.

A firstborn male lamb, "without blemish" was to be prepared for the meal. It represented the sinless life of the Firstborn Son who would die in the prime of His life (Exodus 12:5). The lamb could have no broken bones because none of Christ's bones would be broken when He was executed on the cross (Exodus 12:46; Leviticus 22:24; John 19:32–37). The lamb was to be "roast with fire" representing the cleansing "like fire" that comes to those who take into their lives His whole gospel. All of the roast lamb was to be consumed, "let nothing of it remain," symbolizing the complete way we are to accept Christ into our lives, so much so that we receive His image in our countenances (see Exodus 12:9–10; 3 Nephi 9:20; and Alma 5:14). Just as the ingested lamb became a literal part of them, His teachings were to become an inseparable part of their lives. The meal was also to include unleavened bread because leaven, or yeast, was a symbol of corruption—its absence had reference to Christ's perfect life. Bitter herbs were to be eaten to remind Israel of their bitter bondage in Egypt, representing the sins and evils of the world that spiritually bind us down (Exodus 12:8). The blood from the lamb was to be struck on the door posts of every home, symbolic of the fact that Jesus' atoning blood, pressed from every pore under the weight of the awful Atonement, protects and saves the faithful from spiritual death (D&C 19:16–20; Exodus 12:7). And, the meal was to be kept every spring, when life is renewed, as a memorial and an ordinance forever (Exodus 12:6, 13–14, 17).

It's obvious that every detail of this feast was arranged to bear testimony of the Deliverer. Centuries later, Pilate even presented the Lamb of God to be crucified at the same time the passover lambs were being prepared for slaughter (see John 19:14). The apostle Paul described Christ as "our passover . . . sacrificed for us" (1 Corinthians 5:7–8). Thus, the whole meaning of the law of sacrifice practiced throughout the Old Testament and the Book of Mormon until the coming of Christ in the flesh. "Every whit" of that ceremony pointed "to that great and last sacrifice . . . the Son of God, yea, infinite and eternal," who was our sacrificial Lamb because He offered Himself for our sins (Alma 34:14; Mosiah 14:4–7).

The symbolic meaning and foreshadowed types underlying the Feast of the Passover was completely fulfilled with the Atonement, suffering, death, and resurrection of Jesus. That's why, when Jesus ate the Last Supper with His disciples, the last officially recognized Passover feast, He ended the Passover ordinance and replaced it with a sacramental feast (see Luke 22:1–20). The Passover signified deliverance from death; the sacrament, new life and rebirth. They had the Passover to point their minds forward in time; we now observe the law of the sacrament to point our minds back, to help us remember what He did for us (Luke 22:19–20; D&C 20:77, 79). He no longer requires lambs to be slain in remembrance of His sacrifice but asks for something even more significant: "Thou shalt offer a sacrifice unto the Lord thy God in righteousness, even that of a broken heart and a contrite spirit," the very thing He died from (see D&C 59:8). With a contrite spirit, Jesus humbly submitted His will to the will of His Father, which was to pay the terrible price for our sins and infirmities. The excruciating weight of the Atonement literally caused His heart to burst.[7] Similarly, He now asks us to do the will of the Father and to break our hearts away from the things of this world.

THE PROPHECY OF MICAH (ABOUT 700 BC)
Micah foresaw the city of Christ's birth:

> But thou, Bethlehem Ephratah, though thou be little among the thousands of Judah, yet out of thee shall he come forth unto me that is to be ruler in Israel; whose goings forth have been from of old, from everlasting. (Micah 5:2)

THE PROPHECY OF LEHI (600 BC)
Lehi told his family when the Savior would be born:

Six hundred years from the time [we] left Jerusalem, a prophet [will]
the Lord God raise up among the Jews—even a Messiah, or, in other words,
a Savior of the world. (1 Nephi 10:4)

THE PROPHECY OF NEPHI (BETWEEN 600 AND 592 BC)

Nephi learned of Mary's sacred calling by revelation:

And it came to pass that I [Nephi] looked and beheld the great city
of Jerusalem, and also other cities. And I beheld the city of Nazareth; and
in the city of Nazareth I beheld a virgin, and she was exceedingly fair and
white.

And it came to pass that I saw the heavens open; and an angel came
down and stood before me; and he said unto me: Nephi, what beholdest
thou? And I said unto him: A virgin, most beautiful and fair above all
other virgins. And he said unto me: Knowest thou the condescension of
God? And I said unto him: I know that he loveth his children; nevertheless,
I do not know the meaning of all things. And he said unto me: Behold, the
virgin whom thou seest is the mother of the Son of God, after the manner
of the flesh. (1 Nephi 11:9–18)

To condescend means to "come down." The condescension of God
the Father, Elder Bruce R. McConkie explained, "lies in the fact that
he, an exalted Being, steps down from his eternal throne to become the
Father of a mortal Son, a Son born 'after the manner of the flesh.' Without overstepping the bounds of propriety by saying more than is appropriate, let us say this: God the Almighty; the Maker and Preserver and
Upholder of all things; the Omnipotent One; he by whom the sidereal
heavens came into being, who made the universe and all that therein
is . . . who has a glorified and exalted body, a body of flesh and bones as
tangible as man's; who reigns in equity and justice over the endless billions of his spirit children who inhabit the worlds without number that
roll into being at his word. God the Almighty, who is infinite and eternal,
elects, in his fathomless wisdom, to beget a Son, an Only Son, the Only
Begotten in the flesh."[8]

Nephi continued describing his vision:

And it came to pass that I beheld that she was carried away in the
Spirit; and after she had been carried away in the Spirit for the space of
a time the angel spake unto me, saying: Look! And I looked and beheld
the virgin again, bearing a child in her arms. And the angel said unto

me: Behold the Lamb of God, yea, even the Son of the Eternal Father!
Knowest thou the meaning of the tree [of life] which thy father saw? And
I answered him, saying: Yea, it is the love of God, which sheddeth itself
abroad in the hearts of the children of men; wherefore, it is the most desir-
able above all things. And he spake unto me, saying: Yea, and the most
joyous to the soul.

And after he had said these words, he said unto me: Look! And I looked,
and I beheld the Son of God going forth among the children of men; and I
saw many fall down at his feet and worship him. (1 Nephi 11:19–24)

The tree of eternal life, the tree next to the fountain of living water
that quenches thirst, offers rest to those weary of traveling through the
worldly wilderness. It provides shade and protection from the fiery trials
and heat of the day during our mortal probation, is Jesus Christ (1 Nephi
11:4–7, 20–21). He is the love of God. "For God so loved the world [us],
that he gave his only begotten Son, that whosoever believeth in him
should not perish, but have everlasting life" (John 3:16).

Later, Nephi records, for the first time in all holy writ, the contem-
porary name of the Son of God:

For according to the words of the prophets, the Messiah cometh in six
hundred years from the time that my father left Jerusalem; and according
to the words of the prophets, and also the word of the angel of God, his
name shall be Jesus Christ, the Son of God. (2 Nephi 25:19).

THE PROPHECY OF KING BENJAMIN (124 BC)

King Benjamin learned from an angel of God about the miracles the
Savior would perform as well as the name of the virgin who would bear
the Christ child:

For behold, the time cometh, and is not far distant, that with power, the
Lord Omnipotent who reigneth, who was, and is from all eternity to all eternity,
shall come down from heaven among the children of men, and shall dwell in
a tabernacle of clay, and shall go forth amongst men, working mighty miracles,
such as healing the sick, raising the dead, causing the lame to walk, the blind to
receive their sight, and the deaf to hear, and curing all manner of diseases.

And he shall cast out devils, or the evil spirits which dwell in the hearts
of the children of men.

And lo, he shall suffer temptations, and pain of body, hunger, thirst,
and fatigue, even more than man can suffer, except it be unto death; for
behold, blood cometh from every pore, so great shall be his anguish for the
wickedness and the abominations of his people.

And he shall be called Jesus Christ, the Son of God, the Father of heaven and earth, the Creator of all things from the beginning; and his mother shall be called Mary. (Mosiah 3:5–8)

THE PROPHECY OF ALMA (ABOUT 83 BC)

This is one of the most powerful witnesses of Christ's ministry and empathy. Alma testified that Christ knows everything about us, everything we experience, whether it be pain, sickness, death, infirmity, or sin. He has descended below all so that He can lift us above it all:

I say unto you, that I know of myself that whatsoever I shall say unto you, concerning that which is to come, is true; and I say unto you, that I know that Jesus Christ shall come, yea, the Son, the Only Begotten of the Father, full of grace, and mercy, and truth. And behold, it is he that cometh to take away the sins of the world, yea, the sins of every man who steadfastly believeth on his name.

And now I say unto you that the good shepherd doth call after you; and if you will hearken unto his voice he will bring you into his fold, and ye are his sheep. (Alma 5:48, 60)

But behold, the Spirit hath said this much unto me, saying: Cry unto this people, saying—Repent ye, and prepare the way of the Lord, and walk in his paths, which are straight; for behold, the kingdom of heaven is at hand, and the Son of God cometh upon the face of the earth.

And behold, he shall be born of Mary, at Jerusalem which is the land of our forefathers, she being a virgin, a precious and chosen vessel, who shall be overshadowed and conceive by the power of the Holy Ghost, and bring forth a son, yea, even the Son of God. And he shall go forth, suffering pains and afflictions and temptations of every kind; and this that the word might be fulfilled which saith **he will take upon him the pains and the sicknesses** *of his people.*

And **he will take upon him death**, *that he may loose the bands of death which bind his people; and* **he will take upon him their infirmities**, *that his bowels may be filled with mercy, according to the flesh, that he may know according to the flesh how to succor his people according to their infirmities.*

Now the Spirit knoweth all things; nevertheless the Son of God suffereth according to the flesh that he might **take upon him the sins of his people**, *that he might blot out their transgressions according to the power of his deliverance; and now behold, this is the testimony which is in me.* (Alma 7:9–13; emphasis added)

OTHER PROPHETS TESTIFY

We may not have all their writings, but all prophets have borne witness of Christ. The Old Testament prophets gave so many signs and prophecies about the birth of the Savior that it is hard to imagine how those in Israel watching for their fulfillment could have possibly missed Him. They knew the city He was to be born in, the specific signs to accompany His birth, the great miracles He would perform, the manner of death He would suffer, and myriad other details about His life. They saw the signs, but they were unable to discern their fulfillment in Christ.

One reason for this could be that they failed to distinguish the events that were to occur in their day from the prophesied events that were to take place in the latter days, at the Second Coming. Many misunderstood the mission of the Messiah then, just as many misunderstand the doctrine of His Second Coming now.

Another reason could be that they failed to understand the symbolism used by the Lord in the scriptures. Symbols both conceal and reveal truth, depending on the spiritual maturity of those listening. Alma taught:

> It is given unto many to know the mysteries of God; neverthe-less they are laid under a strict command that they shall not impart only according to the portion of his word which he doth grant unto the children of men, according to the heed and diligence which they give unto him. And therefore, he that will harden his heart, the same receiveth the lesser portion of the word; and he that will not harden his heart, to him is given the greater portion of the word, until it is given unto him to know the mysteries of God until he know them in full. (Alma 12:9–10)

To learn anything, especially the things of the Spirit, requires that a price be paid. Eighty percent
of the word **LEARN**
is **EARN**. That means that a price has to be paid.
And the **EAR** by which
we will **HEAR** the voice of the Lord
is the **HEART**.

When our heart is in tune with the Spirit of the Lord, we can learn more about a symbol. Those Saints who gladly keep commandments have been promised they "shall find wisdom and great treasures of knowledge, even hidden treasures" (D&C 89:19). So perhaps many of those living at the time of Christ's first appearance allowed their hearts to be hardened against the Spirit, making it impossible for them to understand the symbolism of the prophesied signs.

Another possible reason for their veiled understanding could be their rigidity to detail and their obsession with minutia. No question that Jewish commitment to the law is profound, and in a way, they put most other religions to shame with their zealous commitment to the law. But their overcommitment to minutia blinded them and caused them to "look beyond the mark"—when the mark was Christ! (Jacob 4:14). And as a result, their cries of "Hosanna to the Son of David" given in adulation at His triumphal entry into Jerusalem (see Matthew 21:8–9) quickly turned into the tragic screams of "Crucify him, crucify him!" just a few days later (see Matthew 27:22–25). Cataclysmic consequences followed their rejection of the Messiah, for turning their hearts aside and crucifying Christ. Prophets foretold these dire events, and history has confirmed it (see, for example, 2 Nephi 19:13–14 and 25:16).

All of the prophets have known that the Savior's life and ministry did not begin with His birth. Likewise, His ministry did not end with His death. Old Testament scriptures, especially those restored by the Prophet Joseph Smith, teach us many things about the events before His birth and after His death, including Christ's premortal life, divine birth, mortal ministry, Atonement, betrayal, crucifixion, Resurrection, and eternal divinity. We will probably never have a complete list of their prophecies because there are doubtless many records that have been lost, and hopefully, many others yet to come forth.

One of our modern prophets, President Ezra Taft Benson, declared,

> As these inspired prophets rejoiced in the birth and mission of the Savior, so should we. At this sacred season, I wish to add my witness to that of other prophets: the Son of God, even Jesus Christ, lives. He was born and lived in humble circumstances. He ministered among the children of men. He died in holy innocence. He arose from the grave in majesty with His resurrected body. And He will return again to the earth in great triumph and glory. He is indeed our Savior and our Redeemer, the Only Begotten of the Father. And because He lives, so shall we live eternally. May the Babe of Bethlehem be the object of our worship and the focus of our lives during this blessed Christmas season—and always.[9]

Notes

1. Ezra Taft Benson, Christmas Devotional given Dec. 1, 1985; printed in the *LDS Church News*, Dec. 21, 1991, 4.

2. Joseph Fielding Smith, *Conference Report*, Oct. 1967, 121–22.

3. See Elder Neal A. Maxwell, "A Choice Seer," in *Brigham Young University 1985–86 Devotional and Fireside Speeches* [Provo, Utah: University Publications, 1986), 115.

4. In addition to it being used as a sign for Noah, the rainbow has also been designated by the Lord in our day as a sign of the Second Coming. The Prophet Joseph taught, "The Lord deals with this people as a tender parent with a child, communicating light and intelligence and the knowledge of his ways as they can bear it. The inhabitants of the earth are asleep; they know not the day of their visitation. The Lord hath set the bow in the cloud for a sign that while it shall be seen, seed time and harvest, summer and winter shall not fail; but when it shall disappear, woe to that generation, for behold the end cometh quickly" (Joseph Smith, *Teachings of the Prophet Joseph Smith*, sel. Joseph Fielding Smith [Salt Lake City, Utah: Deseret Book, 1976], 305). Later, Joseph Smith further clarified this prophecy: "I have asked of the Lord concerning His coming; and while asking the Lord, He gave a sign and said, 'In the days of Noah I set a bow in the heavens as a sign and token that in any year that the bow should be seen the Lord would not come; but there should be seed time and harvest during that year: but whenever you see the bow withdrawn, it shall be a token that there shall be famine, pestilence, and great distress among the nations, and that the coming of the Messiah is not far distant' " (Joseph Smith, *Teachings of the Prophet Joseph Smith*, sel. Joseph Fielding Smith [Salt Lake City, Utah: Deseret Book, 1976], 340–41).

5. Joseph Smith, *Teachings of the Prophet Joseph Smith*, sel. Joseph Fielding Smith [Salt Lake City: Deseret Book, 1976], 157.

6. See George Reynolds, "The Jaredites," *Juvenile Instructor*, 27 (May 1, 1892): 282. See also Stella Cahoon Shurtleff and Brent Farrington Cahoon, comps., *Reynolds Cahoon and his Stalwart Sons*, 1960, 21.

7. See James E. Talmage, *Jesus the Christ* (Salt Lake City: Deseret Book, 1977), 668–69.

8. Bruce R. McConkie, *The Mortal Messiah*, 4 vols. (Salt Lake City: Deseret Book, 1979), 1:314–15.

9. Ezra Taft Benson, First Presidency Christmas devotional, Dec. 4, 1988; quoted in the *LDS Church News*, Dec. 21, 1991, 4.

FIVE

Unto Us a Child Is Born

ALL OF THE ANCIENT PROPHETS foretold of the coming of the Christ because His birth was the Messianic Hope and Promise of "peace on earth." And of their recorded testimonies and writings, none were greater than Isaiah's. He is the most quoted prophet in the Book of Mormon and the prophet most often quoted by the Savior Himself. Isaiah's writings are quoted more in the Doctrine and Covenants and in the New Testament than any other prophet. He was also the most quoted author in all subsequent Jewish literature. It's no surprise that the Savior has commanded us to "search Isaiah diligently" (see 3 Nephi 20:11–12, 23:1–3; Mormon 8:22–23; 1 Nephi 19:23–24; 2 Nephi 6:4, 11:2; 25:8).

One of the most compelling reasons to study Isaiah's writings is because he knew Christ (2 Nephi 11:2). Nephi declared, "That I might more fully persuade [my family] to believe in the Lord their Redeemer, I did read unto them that which was written by the prophet Isaiah" (1 Nephi 19:23).

Foretelling Christ's birth seven hundred years before it occurred, Isaiah wrote: "*Therefore, the Lord himself shall give you a sign—Behold, a virgin shall conceive, and shall bear a son, and shall call his name Immanuel*" (meaning "with us is God"; 2 Nephi 17:14).

This passage is cited in the New Testament by Matthew as being fulfilled with the birth of Jesus Christ (see Matthew 1:25). The Book of

Mormon, a second witness for Christ and for the Bible, reaffirms Isaiah's ancient prophecy, that it was indeed a virgin who would conceive and bear the Son of God (see 1 Nephi 11:13, 15, 18, 20–21). And speaking of Isaiah's profound and truthful declaration, President Marion G. Romney said:

> Here is another example in which men revise the scriptures without the inspiration of the spirit. Isaiah, in predicting the birth of Christ, said: "Behold, a *virgin* shall conceive, and bear a son, and shall call his name Immanuel." When Isaiah used the word *virgin*, he was saying that a woman who had not known a man should bear a son. The modern translators say: "Behold a *young woman* shall conceive and bear a son, and shall call his name Immanuel" (Revised Standard Version of the Bible[1]). You see, they do not believe that Christ was divine, so it does not make any difference to them whether they say a *young woman* or a *virgin*."[2]

Isaiah further testified of the divinity of Christ's birth by listing some of the sacred names and titles by which the Babe of Bethlehem would be known: *"For unto us a child is born, unto us a son is given; and the government shall be upon his shoulder; and his name shall be called, Wonderful, Counselor, The Mighty God, The Everlasting Father, The Prince of Peace. Of the increase of government and peace there is no end, upon the throne of David, and upon his kingdom to order it, and to establish it with judgment and with justice from henceforth, even forever"* (2 Nephi 19:6–7).[3]

Why do the scriptures consistently refer to the Son as "the Mighty God" and the "the Everlasting Father"? How are Jesus and the Father one? Christ "is in the Father," meaning He looks like the Father; He speaks the words the Father would speak if the Father were there Himself; He put the Father's plan into operation; He created the worlds the Father instructed Him to organize; and He allowed His will to be "swallowed up in the will of the Father" by permitting Himself to be "led, crucified, and slain" (see D&C 93:5 and Mosiah 15:2, 5–8). The Father is "in Christ" because He is Christ's literal father; because He passed on to Christ His own attributes, nature, and character; and because He gave Christ "of his fulness," all the power, authority and dominion He, Himself, holds (see D&C 93:4–5 and Mosiah 15:3–4). The Father and the Son are one in every way, except one—they are two separate, distinct beings.

The inspired writings of Isaiah about the birth of the Messiah have been a source of great inspiration to many people. Composer George Frederick Handel was particularly moved by the passages in Isaiah. In just twenty-three days he wrote over fifty separate pieces of music that have since come to be the world's most popular Christmas oratorio: *Messiah*. Almost all of the text for this masterpiece comes from the writings of Isaiah. The story of Handel's *Messiah* and its impact on the author and the world has been described by Jay Welch, former Assistant Director of the Mormon Tabernacle Choir:

> On the right day in London of the 1740s you could see him walking down Brook Street in the vicinity of Grosvenor Square. An elderly gentleman, neatly dressed in his lace coat, ruffles and three-cornered hat, he would proceed at full steam, talking to himself as if the problems of the nation were on his shoulders, and then pause abruptly to contemplate his surroundings. The people he passed often noticed that he spoke a mixture of two languages. He was the greatest composer England ever had, though he was an adopted one from Germany.
>
> If you had followed this curious cosmopolitan gentleman along Brook Street to his home on August 22, 1741, you might have seen him sit at his desk in the front room and start to put notes on paper with remarkable speed. For the next 23 days he wouldn't leave the house; his manservant would bring his meals to the room. Then, on September 14, after a little over three weeks of feverish work on the manuscript, he would shut the completed "Messiah" in his drawer where it would remain practically untouched for the next seven weeks!
>
> Whatever the case, we know that Handel was deeply moved during the 23 days. At one point, after having written down the Hallelujah Chorus, he called to his manservant and with eyes filled with tears exclaimed, "I did think I did see all heaven before me, and the great God Himself."
>
> Handel, like Bach had been raised in the solid, strict atmosphere of Protestant Germany, and he was a man of great personal religion. His pocket book, kept slim by the social (not musical) failure of his theatrical ventures, was made slimmer by his constant devotion to several charities in town. His favorite charity was the Founding Hospital, an institution for homeless and maltreated children of London, and it is here that he started a tradition of annual benefit performances of "Messiah" a few years before his death.
>
> Four days before the scheduled premiere of "Messiah," Handel conducted a public rehearsal of it which drew this high praise from Faulkner's personal Journal: "It was allowed by the greatest Judges to be the finest Composition of Musick that ever was heard . . . ." The actual first performance took place on April 13, 1742, one day later

than announced, before a record audience of some 700 persons in a hall designed to accommodate only 600. Room for the additional 100 persons was made through the cooperative response of all concerned to a newspaper notice requesting that the ladies leave their hoops at home and the gentlemen, their swords. Handel presided at the organ.

Little more need be said about this great oratorio except that following the premiere, Handel conducted another performance of it in Ireland before he brought it back to England. It was at the English premiere in Covent Garden in March 1743, that King George II, so moved at the inspiration of the Hallelujah Chorus that he arose to hear the remainder of it, inaugurated the tradition of standing during its performance.

Through the music of "Messiah" we participate, in a new way, in the life of the Savior. At the outset we are identified with the prophets who speak. When the chorus sings "For unto us a Child is born," we are no longer prophets but shepherds with them. And when the strains of the Pastoral Symphony reach our ears, we, too, offer up a lullaby to the new-born King. Indeed, through Handel's music, in a unique way, the Messiah of the World is "made flesh, and walks among us."[4]

Notes

1. Holy Bible, Revised Standard Version (New York: Thomas Nelson and Sons, 1952); Isaiah 7:14.

2. Marion G. Romney, in Conference Report, Tokyo Japan Area Conference, 1975, 46.

3. This verse is from Isaiah 9:6. I used the Book of Mormon reference because in its rendering, *mighty* and *everlasting* are capitalized.

4. From the inside cover of the Mormon Tabernacle Choir album *Messiah*; notes by Dr. Jay Welch, Assistant Director, Tabernacle Choir.

SIX

"FIVE YEARS MORE . . .

Then Cometh the Son of God"

JUST FIVE YEARS BEFORE THE birth of the Messiah in Bethlehem, the Lord called a Lamanite prophet named Samuel to testify to the Nephites in the Americas of the signs that would accompany that glorious event. Samuel predicted the signs, bore testimony that Christ would redeem men from temporal and spiritual death, and foretold the signs of His death, including three days of darkness, the rending of rocks, and great upheavals of nature.

> *And now it came to pass that Samuel, the Lamanite, did prophesy a great many more things which cannot be written. And behold, he said unto them: Behold, I give unto you a sign.* (Helaman 14:1–2)

Certain heavenly phenomena are sometimes designated as signs, in order that their promised occurrence will stand as a witness of the prophesied event. "In every age the Lord sends forth clearly discernible signs and warnings so that those who are spiritually inclined can know of his hand-dealings with men."[1] As the prophet Amos declared, "Surely the Lord God will do nothing *until* he revealeth his secret unto his servants the prophets" (JST, Amos 3:7; emphasis added).

Samuel not only foretold the signs, but he also declared to the Nephites the time when those signs would be fulfilled: "

For five years more cometh, and behold, then cometh the Son of God
to redeem all those who shall believe on his name. And behold, this will I
give unto you for a sign at the time of his coming; for behold, there shall be
great lights in heaven. (Helaman 14:2)

Christ is the Light of the World (see John 8:12). How appropriate to
have darkness banished as a sign of His birth (see 3 Nephi 1:15, 19).

Great lights have been seen in the heavens on many different occasions.[2] Greater signs and wonders already have and will yet be shown
in the heavens and on the earth to those living in the latter days (see
D&C 29:14, 45:40). In our own time, for instance, on a Sunday evening (November 15, 1981) the night before the Jordan River Temple was
dedicated, the heavens in the Salt Lake Valley were ablaze with burning
crimson colors of pink and gold, as if the clouds themselves were bearing witness of the glorious event to take place the next day. The newly
called temple workers were meeting in a chapel in South Jordan, Utah,
for instructions. As they came outside, they were greeted not only by the
brilliantly lit sky but a brightly colored rainbow whose very end came to
rest on the statue of the Angel Moroni on the tower of the Jordan River
Temple just a few blocks away. One of them remarked, "The temple is the
pot of gold at the end of the rainbow." Several took photographs. Cars
stopped alongside roads. People looked on in reverent awe.

Meteorologists stated that the cause of the spectacular sunset that
evening was caused by the ash that had been thrown into the atmosphere
by a volcanic eruption in Mexico a year earlier. The volcano effect! Perhaps so, but those with eyes to see, and hearts to feel and understand,
knew that there was a special light and glory reflecting across those perfectly aligned clouds that particular Sunday evening. Nothing spiritual is
ever a coincidence.

Samuel continued his prophecy to the Nephites:

For behold, there shall be great lights in heaven, insomuch that in the
night before he cometh there shall be no darkness, insomuch that it shall
appear unto man as if it was day.

Therefore, there shall be one day and a night and a day, as if it were
one day and there were no night; and this shall be unto you for a sign; for
ye shall know of the rising of the sun and also of its setting; therefore they
shall know of a surety that there shall be two days and a night; nevertheless
the night shall not be darkened; and it shall be the night before he is born.
(Helaman 14:3–4)

Imagine hearing such a prophecy! If you had heard Samuel make that prediction and then saw it fulfilled five years later, would you have believed? The Nephites actually saw it take place, yet many of them rationalized it away. "The volcano effect! That's all it is!" Too often mortals rationalize and try to explain away the hand of the Lord when it is made manifest in their lives.

Samuel now foretold of another sign. At the birth of Him who is called the "bright and morning star" (see Revelation 22:16), it was prophesied that a new star would appear in the heavens (see Matthew 2:2, 7, 9; 3 Nephi 1:21).[3]

> *And behold, there shall a new star arise, such an one as ye never have beheld; and this also shall be a sign unto you.*
>
> *And behold this is not all, there shall be many signs and wonders in heaven. And it shall come to pass that ye shall all be amazed, and wonder, insomuch that ye shall fall to the earth.*
>
> *And it shall come to pass that whosoever shall believe on the Son of God, the same shall have everlasting life.*
>
> *And behold, thus hath the Lord commanded me, by his angel, that I should come and tell this thing unto you; yea, he hath commanded that I should prophesy these things unto you; yea, he hath said unto me: Cry unto this people, repent and prepare the way of the Lord.* (Helaman 14:5–9)

WHOSOEVER WILL BELIEVE WILL BE SAVED

Worldly people, rather than those who humble themselves and repent, choose to fight against the Lord's prophets. Whether those prophets are raised nearby or come from a distant place, they, like the Lord Himself, have all faced disappointment and discouragement trying to teach people truth (see Luke 4:16–30; Alma 8:9–15). Samuel the Lamanite was treated like most prophets are by the world. He told his people,

> *And now, because I am a Lamanite, and have spoken unto you the words which the Lord hath commanded me, and because it was hard against you, ye are angry with me and do seek to destroy me, and have cast me out from among you.* (Helaman 14:10)

An increase of love and tolerance, understanding and respect toward one another is needed among people of all faiths. But it is especially tragic when the house of Israel rejects their own prophets. The character assassination and religious hatred that are spawned by the seething spirit, vicious falsehoods, libelous histories, and odious nonsense of unreasonable prejudice is evidence that Satan has "gotten great hold upon the hearts of the people . . . therefore they would not hearken unto the words" of the prophets sent to them (see Alma 8:9–11; D&C 123:4–7). Instead, they harden their hearts, close their minds, and argue and fight (see Moses 6:37–38; 7:12–13).

The reasons the Lord sends prophets to foretell future signs and events were clearly stated by Samuel when he appeared among the Nephites (see italicized passages below). Signs don't give us faith, but knowing the words of the prophets and seeing them fulfilled can strengthen the faithful:

> *And ye shall hear my words, for, for this intent have I come up upon the walls of this city,* **that ye might hear and know of the judgments of God** *which do await you because of your iniquities, and also* **that ye might know the conditions of repentance;**
>
> *And also* **that ye might know of the coming of Jesus Christ,** *the Son of God, the Father of heaven and of earth, the Creator of all things from the beginning; and* **that ye might know of the signs of his coming, to the intent that ye might believe on his name.**
>
> *And if ye believe on his name* **ye will repent of all your sins, that thereby ye may have a remission of them** *through his merits.* (Helaman 14:11–13; emphasis added)
>
> *. . . And the angel said unto me that many shall see greater things than these, to the intent that they might believe that these signs and these wonders should come to pass upon all the face of this land, to the intent* **that there should be no cause for unbelief** *among the children of men—*
>
> *And this to the intent* **that whosoever will believe might be saved, and that whosoever will not believe, a righteous judgment might come upon them;** *and also if they are condemned they bring upon themselves their own condemnation.*
>
> *And now remember, remember, my brethren, that whosoever perisheth, perisheth unto himself; and whosoever doeth iniquity, doeth it unto himself; for behold, ye are free; ye are permitted to act for yourselves; for behold,* **God hath given unto you a knowledge** *and he hath made you free.*
>
> *He hath given unto you that ye might know good from evil, and he hath given unto you that ye might choose life or death; and ye can do good and be restored unto that which is good, or have that which is good restored unto you; or ye can do evil, and have that which is evil restored unto you.* (Helaman 14:28–31; emphasis added)

Unfortunately, like most prophetic warnings, Samuel's prophecies were rejected by the majority of the people. The negative reaction to Samuel the Lamanite is typical, even today. Prophets don't always tell us what we want to know, but what we need to know. That's why these events in the Book of Mormon read like a current edition of the daily newspaper. They were written by prophets who saw our society in vision, who witnessed similar events in their own day, and whose hearts yearned to help us succeed. They prayed that we would "learn to be more wise than [they had] been" (Mormon 9:31). And as we read of their experiences, we develop a profound sense of gratitude for their concern for our welfare. President Ezra Taft Benson affirmed, "The Book of Mormon was written for us today. God is the author of the book. It is a record of a fallen people, compiled by inspired men for our blessing today. Those people never had the book—it was meant for us. Mormon, the ancient prophet after whom the book is named, abridged centuries of records. God, who knows the end from the beginning, told him what to include in his abridgement that we would need for our day."[4]

Some may wonder why the Lord doesn't call more prophets, or why prophets are often older. Interesting that we often are out of breath just trying to *lengthen our stride, quicken our pace, extend our reach,* and *increase our vision* in order to keep up with them, despite their age. With age comes wisdom. Are we wise enough to follow those blessed with wisdom? "What we need today," President Harold B. Lee declared, "is not more prophets. We have the prophets. But what we need is more people with listening ears. That is the great need of our generation."[5]

One of the evidences that a society is fully ripened in iniquity is that they persecute and then cast out the humble prophets of God. And when maligning beliefs, sensational and unsubstantiated rumors, and an incendiary arsenal of religious bigotry fails to find its mark, the only option left, the wicked assume, is to permanently silence the seers. Gratefully, however, there are always some in every dispensation who have ears to hear and hearts that understand the testimony of living prophets:

> And now, it came to pass that there were many who heard the words of Samuel, the Lamanite, which he spake upon the walls of the city. And as many as believed on his word went forth and sought for Nephi; and when they had come forth and found him they confessed unto him their sins and denied not, desiring that they might be baptized unto the Lord.

But as many as there were who did not believe in the words of Samuel were angry with him; and they cast stones at him upon the wall, and also many shot arrows at him as he stood upon the wall; but the Spirit of the Lord was with him, insomuch that they could not hit him with their stones neither with their arrows. Now when they saw that they could not hit him, there were many more who did believe on his words, insomuch that they went away unto Nephi to be baptized.

For behold, Nephi was baptizing, and prophesying, and preaching, crying repentance unto the people, showing signs and wonders, working miracles among the people, that they might know that the Christ must shortly come—telling them of things which must shortly come, that they might know and remember at the time of their coming that they had been made known unto them beforehand, to the intent that they might believe; therefore as many as believed on the words of Samuel went forth unto him to be baptized, for they came repenting and confessing their sins.

But the more part of them did not believe in the words of Samuel; therefore when they saw that they could not hit him with their stones and their arrows, they cried unto their captains, saying: Take this fellow and bind him, for behold he hath a devil; and because of the power of the devil which is in him we cannot hit him with our stones and our arrows; therefore take him and bind him, and away with him. And as they went forth to lay their hands on him, behold, he did cast himself down from the wall, and did flee out of their lands, yea, even unto his own country, and began to preach and to prophesy among his own people. And behold, he was never heard of more among the Nephites; and thus were the affairs of the people.
(Helaman 16:1–8)

A PATTERN FOR THE SECOND COMING

As we ponder these scriptures, it becomes obvious that the first coming of Christ to the earth at Bethlehem, as experienced by the Nephites in America, is a pattern or type, in many respects, of His glorious Second Coming in the last days.[6] Some of the signs given to the Jewish nation in Israel, and some of the signs given to the Nephites and Lamanites in the Americas, will also be shown again prior to the Second Coming.

Anyone who will carefully read the Book of Mormon will see dramatic types of our government, society, wars, and Church. President Ezra Taft Benson has said, "The record of the Nephite history just prior to the Savior's visit reveals many parallels to our own day as we anticipate the Savior's Second Coming."[7] "In the Book of Mormon we find a pattern for preparing for the Second Coming. A major portion of the book centers on the few decades just prior to Christ's coming to America. By careful study of that time period, we can determine why some were destroyed in the terrible judgments that preceded His coming and what brought others to stand at the temple in the land of Bountiful and thrust their hands into the wounds of His hands and feet."[8]

A careful study of the occurrences preceding and attending the Savior's first coming offers a striking similarity to the prophesied events of the Second Coming. As we read about His appearance we can experience vicariously what transpired in Jerusalem and in ancient America. We become painfully aware of their remorse for not having distinguished the signs more carefully and trust that we will be more conscientious of the signs of His Second Coming given in our own day.

> And in one place they were heard to cry, saying: O that we had repented before this great and terrible day, and then would our brethren have been spared, and they would not have been burned in that great city Zarahemla.
>
> And in another place they were heard to cry and mourn, saying: O that we had repented before this great and terrible day, and had not killed and stoned the prophets, and cast them out; then would our mothers and our fair daughters, and our children have been spared, and not have been buried up in that great city Moronihah.
>
> And thus were the howlings of the people great and terrible. (3 Nephi 8:24–25)

In their anguish we discover a pattern of procrastination that can hopefully serve as a key to help us be better prepared for the Second Coming of the Lord. Some may think, "I have never stoned or killed the prophets. This doesn't apply to me!" Most often people cast prophets out of their hearts long before their countries do. And that can include something as simple as refusing to follow the living prophets, favoring the counsel of prophets who have long since passed away. We should remember that it is possible to mentally stone the prophets and cast them out of our lives by failing to read and follow their messages. The most important book of scripture we could read might well be the most recent report of general conference. Elder Spencer W. Kimball pointedly asked, "Do you also build sepulchers for the dead prophets and tombs for those who have passed away long ago and disregard the living ones?"[9] "Even in this Church many are prone to garnish the sepulchres of yesterday's prophets and mentally stone the living ones."[10]

Speaking on this same point, President Harold B. Lee shared an analogy of how we can have safely avoid the anguish experienced by the Nephites:

> Some months ago, millions of watchers and listeners over the world waited breathlessly and anxiously the precarious flight of Apollo 13. The whole world, it seemed, prayed for one significant result: the safe return to earth of three brave men.
>
> When one of them with restrained anxiety announced the startling information, "We have an explosion!" The mission control in Houston immediately mobilized all the technically trained scientists who had, over the years, planned every conceivable detail pertaining to that flight.
>
> The safety of those three now depended on two vital qualifications: on the reliability of the skills and the knowledge of those technicians in the mission control center at Houston, and upon the implicit obedience of the men in the Aquarius to every instruction from the technicians, who, because of their understanding of the problems of the astronauts, were better qualified to find the essential solutions. The decisions of the technicians had to be perfect or the Aquarius could have missed the earth by thousands of miles.
>
> This dramatic event is somewhat analogous to these troubled times in which we live. The headlines in the public press only this week made another startling announcement by a presidential commission to the President of the United States. "U.S. Society Is in Peril." Many are frightened when they see and hear of unbelievable happenings the world over—political intrigues, wars and contention everywhere, frustrations of parents, endeavoring to cope with social problems that threaten to break down the sanctity of the home, the frustrations of children and youth as they face challenges to their faith and their morals.
>
> Only if you are willing to listen and obey as did the astronauts on the Aquarius, can you and all your households be guided to ultimate safety and security in the Lord's own way.
>
> There are in these troubled times, agonizing cries of distress among the people of the earth. There are intense feelings of a need for some way to find a solution to overwhelming problems and to ease this distress from all that affects mankind.[11]

As Elder Maxwell wisely observed, "We are entering times wherein there will be for all of us as Church members, in my judgment, some special challenges which will require of us that we follow the Brethren. All the easy things that the Church has had to do have been done. From now on, it's high adventure, and fellowship is going to be tested in some interesting ways."[12]

With the guidance of living prophets, and by the power of the Holy Ghost, faithful Saints are able to discern the signs and the times of the signs which are a prophesied part of this final great dispensation preparatory to the Second Coming (see D&C 39:23). Wisely, we should choose to willingly follow the Brethren so that we can be better prepared to receive the Savior in these latter days.

Notes

1. Bruce R. McConkie, *Mormon Doctrine*, 2nd ed. (Salt Lake City: Bookcraft, 1966), 715.

2. Joseph Smith, Heber C. Kimball, and others have witnessed glorious lights and other signs in the heavens. See *History of the Church*, 4:439; 5:301, 309–311; and Orson F. Whitney's *Life of Heber C. Kimball* (Salt Lake City: Bookcraft, 1945), 31–33.

3. See *The Growing Edge*, Church Education System monthly newsletter, vol. 14 (Dec. 1981).

4. See Ezra Taft Benson, in Conference Report, Apr. 1975, 94.

5. Harold B. Lee, paraphrasing J. Reuben Clark Jr.'s conference address (see Conference Report, Oct. 1948, 82) as found in "The Place of the Living Prophet, Seer, and Revelator," address to Seminary and Institute of Religion faculty, Brigham Young University, July 8, 1964, typescript, Church Historical Department, Salt Lake City, Utah, 9.

6. Elder Delbert L. Stapley has observed, "The pressure of Satan's power is intensified as the time of the Savior's Second Coming to earth draws near. We have a foreboding example as recorded in the Book of Mormon history of the Nephite people in the years just preceding the birth of Christ into the world. Samuel, the Lamanite Prophet, prophesied to the Nephites of the approaching birth of Jesus Christ, our Lord, in the land of Jerusalem. They rejected his witness and testimony. They attempted to explain away the teachings of Samuel and the unusual phenomena of nature so much in evidence on this continent before Christ's birth, which happenings were also prophesied of by their prophets. They accused their spiritual leaders of keeping the people down to be servants to their words, also servants to them. Thus ignorantly persuaded they were willing to yield themselves to the

teachings and warnings of the prophets (in Conference Report, Oct. 1961, 21).

7. See Ezra Taft Benson, *A Witness and a Warning* (Salt Lake City, Utah: Deseret Book, 1988), 37.

8. See Ezra Taft Benson, in Conference Report, Oct. 1986, 5.

9. Spencer W. Kimball, in Conference Report, Oct. 1949, 123.

10. Spencer W. Kimball, "To His Servants the Prophets," *Instructor Magazine*, 95 (August 1960): 257.

11. Harold B. Lee, in Conference Report, Oct. 1970, 113–14.

12. Neal A. Maxwell, "The Old Testament: Relevancy Within Antiquity," *The Third Annual Church Educational System Religious Educators' Symposium,* Brigham Young University, Aug. 18, 1979 (Salt Lake City: The Church of Jesus Christ of Latter-day Saints), 12.

SEVEN

THE FORERUNNER

Who Prepared the Way

I N PALESTINE, THE JEWISH NATION was in a state of apostasy and great wickedness. Almost two thousand years earlier, Jacob, in blessing his twelve sons, had promised Judah, "The scepter shall not depart from Judah, nor a lawgiver from between his feet, until Shiloh (meaning "He to whom it belongs") come" to preside over his people (Genesis 49:10; JST, Genesis 50:24). Even though Judah was under the domination of foreign nations for centuries after her fall to Babylon in 587 BC, all of the local rulers of the Jews were of the tribe of Judah until the days drew near for Jesus to be born.

Herod was the first foreigner in over two thousand years to sit on the Jewish throne, fulfilling the patriarchal and prophetic blessing given to Judah. And Christ was born in the last year of Herod's reign. Truly, the scepter had not departed from Judah until Shiloh had come. By his marriage with Mariamne, Herod the Great allied himself with the family of the Maccabees, who had been for several generations the leaders of the patriotic party among the Jews.[1] Herod was not qualified to reign because he was not of the house of David (he was a descendant of Esau). But he had demonstrated such great loyalty to Rome that he was appointed a client-king over Judea by his close friend Caesar Augustus, the first emperor of the Roman Empire.

Herod became famous throughout the empire for his massive construction programs, which earned him the nickname of "Great Builder" or "Herod the Great." Herod's promotion of pagan temples and Greek culture in the land of Israel so infuriated the Jewish people that he erected a large shrine over the burial cave of Abraham, Isaac, and Jacob in an attempt to calm their anger and gain their favor. He also rebuilt the temple of Solomon at an immense cost. Over ten thousand craftsmen and one thousand priests were assembled to labor on the monumental project. It took only nine years to complete the temple, but eighty-four additional years to construct the associated complex of magnificent courtyards, buildings, and stunning Royal Portico of Corinthian columns. A popular saying among the people was, "Whoever has not seen Herod's Temple has never seen anything beautiful."[2]

Although the temple was beautiful, its leadership was corrupt. The sacred office of high priest was no longer in the hands of one who held the keys of the Aaronic Priesthood. And though Herod's buildings were splendid, "his reign was disgraced by many acts of cruelty. In a fit of jealousy he had his wife, whom he dearly loved, put to death; later on he had her two sons Alexander and Aristobulus, also murdered. In the same year in which he gave the order for the massacre of the infants at Bethlehem, he had Antipater, another of his own sons, put to death. A few months later Herod himself died."[3] Elder James E. Talmage adds this note about Herod's character:

> Herod was professedly an adherent of the religion of Judah, though by birth an Idumean, by descent an Edomite or one of the posterity of Esau, all of whom the Jews hated; and of all Edomites not one was more bitterly detested than was Herod the king. He was tyrannical and merciless, sparing neither foe nor friend who came under suspicion of being a possible hindrance to his ambitious designs. He had his wife and several of his sons, as well as others of his blood kindred, cruelly murdered; and he put to death nearly all of the great national council, the Sanhedrin. His reign was one of revolting cruelty and unbridled oppression. Only when in danger of inciting a national revolt or in fear of incurring the displeasure of his imperial master, the Roman emperor, did he stay his hand in any undertaking.[4]

This is the Herod that Luke referred to in his account of the Savior's birth.

> *There was in the days of Herod, the king of Judea, a certain priest named Zacharias, of the course of Abia; and his wife being of the daughters of Aaron, and her name Elizabeth.* (JST, Luke 1:5)

There were many priests in Israel in Zacharias's day—between twenty thousand and twenty-four thousand of them, who, like Zacharias and Elizabeth, were lineal descendants of Aaron—whose right it was to officiate in the sacrifices that were made in similitude of the eternal sacrifice of their expected Deliverer. King David had divided the priests into twenty-four groups or courses (see 1 Chronicles 24:10). Each family leader became the ancestral head of their lineage. Only four courses (or family lines) of priests returned to Jerusalem from the Babylonian captivity. Unfortunately, most of these priestly descendants were now corrupt. "It was a day when the priestly office, once held by Aaron's worthy sons, was now held by their unworthy descendants. Pride, disbelief, dishonesty, violence, immorality, and even the shedding of blood—all these prevailed and were more common than not among those who should have been lights to the people. Few of the priests envisioned to any real degree the true significance of the sacred ordinances it was their privilege to perform."[5]

Twice each year, in April and October, the priests of the course of Abia (named for Abijah, see Ezra 2:36–39) traveled from their homes to the temple in Jerusalem to take their week-long turns at performing the sacred rites and ordinances that had been the center of Israel's worship for fifteen hundred years. It was October, the autumn of the year, when Zacharias left his home in Hebron to travel some twenty miles to Jerusalem. The lot that fell to him that year entitled him to officiate in the Holy of Holies in the temple, a privilege of such magnitude that it probably only came once in a priest's entire lifetime.

"THIS IS ELIAS, WHOM I SEND TO PREPARE THE WAY BEFORE ME"

Zacharias and Elizabeth were exceptions to the wickedness of the day. Yet, in spite of their righteousness, Elizabeth had born them no children and they were now "well stricken in years":

> [They] were both righteous before God, walking in all the commandments and ordinances of the Lord blameless; And they had no child. Elizabeth was barren, and they were both well stricken in years.
>
> And while he executed the priest's office before God, in the order of his priesthood. According to the law, [his lot was to burn incense when he went into the temple of the Lord]. The whole multitude of the people were praying without at the time of incense. And there appeared unto him an angel of the Lord, standing on the right side of the altar of incense. (JST, Luke 1:6–11)

Zacharias's personal worthiness is illustrated by the experience itself. Angels can appear to anyone at any time, but they "*do not minister* unto carnal and godless souls; it is those who seek, by righteousness, the blessings of heaven who are permitted to see within the veil."[6]

> *And when Zacharias saw the angel, he was troubled and fear fell upon him.*
>
> *But the angel said unto him, Fear not, Zacharias, for thy prayer is heard, and thy wife Elizabeth shall bear thee a son, and thou shalt call his name John.*
>
> *Thou shalt have joy and gladness, and many shall rejoice at his birth;*
>
> *For he shall be great in the sight of the Lord, and shall drink neither wine nor strong drink.* (JST, Luke 1:12–15)

The announcement of the angel serves to remind us never to assume that because a home has not been blessed with children it is therefore somehow "cursed." Children, and many other blessings from the Lord, are never denied the righteous. Sometimes they are delayed, for whatever purposes the Lord sees fit, according to His will, but never ultimately denied.

John's birth was to be a sign to all Israel that the Messiah, the Consolation of Israel, would soon come. John would live as a Nazarite, meaning he was a "man under a vow to abstain from wine, from any cutting of the hair, and any contact with the dead. The vow might be lifelong, or for a short definite period."[7] The word *Nazarite* means "a consecrated man." John was consecrated and set apart for his special mission, even before his birth, to be the forerunner who would prepare the way for the Messiah.

In 1832, the Prophet Joseph Smith received a revelation confirming the significance of John's mission. The Lord revealed that because ancient Israel had failed to prepare themselves, He had taken Moses, the Holy (Melchizedek) Priesthood, and the ordinances of the temple out of their midst (see D&C 84:18–25; JST, Exodus 34:1–2; JST, Deuteronomy 10:1–2).

> And the lesser priesthood continued, which priesthood holdeth the key of the ministering of angels and the preparatory gospel; Which gospel is the gospel of repentance and of baptism, and the remission of sins, and the law of carnal commandments, which the Lord in his wrath caused to continue with the house of Aaron among the children of Israel until John, whom God raised up, being filled with the Holy Ghost from his mother's womb.

For he was baptized while he was yet in his childhood, and was ordained by the angel of God at the time he was eight days old unto this power, to overthrow the kingdom of the Jews, and to make straight the way of the Lord before the face of his people, to prepare them for the coming of the Lord, in whose hand is given all power. (D&C 84:26–28)

John's birth was also a miraculous conception. Not in the sense that Mary's was, but because John's mother, Elizabeth, was well beyond child-bearing age. Zacharias was next told by the angel Gabriel about the effect his son's mission would have on Israel. This may have been the most important announcement Zacharias had heard:

> And he shall be filled with the Holy Ghost, even from his mother's womb. And many of the children of Israel shall he turn to the Lord their God; And he shall go before the Lord in the spirit and power of Elias [as a forerunner to prepare the way], to turn the hearts of the fathers to the children, and the disobedient [the Jewish religious leaders] to the wisdom of the just [the Old Testament Patriarchs], to make ready a people prepared for the Lord. (JST, Luke 1:15–17)

Overwhelmed by the angel's message, Zacharias wondered how it would be possible. Elizabeth couldn't have children, and to have a child so special was too much for even Zacharias' great faith.

> And Zacharias said unto the angel, Whereby shall I know this? for I am an old man, and my wife is well stricken in years.
> And the angel answering, said unto him, I am Gabriel, who stand in the presence of God, and am sent to speak unto thee, and to show thee these glad tidings. (JST, Luke 1:18–19)

Gabriel is Noah, and he "stands next in authority to Adam in the Priesthood."[8] So "what could be more fitting, then," Elder McConkie observed, "than for Michael or Adam, who presides over the angels and directs their labors, to send Gabriel, his next in command, to announce to the mortals involved those things they needed to know concerning the Promised Messiah and his Elias?"[9] It is also interesting to note that the very prophet who witnessed the destruction of the world in the great flood was the one chosen to return to the earth and announce the birth of the Redeemer of all mankind!

But because Zacharias doubted, he was given a sign:

And behold, thou shalt be dumb, and not able to speak until the day that these things shall be performed, because thou believest not my words which shall be fulfilled in their season. (JST, Luke 1:20)

Zacharias had asked a strong and mighty angel, sent from the presence of God, for a sign, and he got one! But it wasn't what he had expected. Speaking of an incident that took place with a sign seeker in Joseph Smith's lifetime, Elder George A. Smith said that when The Church of Jesus Christ of Latter-day Saints was first founded, "you could see persons rise up and ask, 'What sign will you show us that we may be made to believe?' " Elder Smith continued:

A preacher named Hayden introduced himself saying that he had come a considerable distance to be convinced of the truth. "Why," said he, "Mr. Smith, I want to know the truth, and when I am convinced, I will spend all my talents and time in defending and spreading the doctrines of your religion, and I will give you to understand that to convince me is equivalent to convincing all my society, amounting to several hundreds." Well, Joseph commenced laying before him the coming forth of the work, and the first principles of the Gospel, when Mr. Hayden exclaimed, "O this is not the evidence I want, the evidence that I wish to have is a notable miracle; I want to see some powerful manifestation of the power of God, I want to see a notable miracle performed; and if you perform such a one, then I will believe with all my heart and soul and will exert all my power and all my extensive influence to convince others; and if you will not perform a miracle of this kind, then I am your worst and bitterest enemy."

"Well," said Joseph, "what will you have done? Will you be struck blind, or dumb? Will you be paralyzed, or will you have one hand withered? Take your choice, choose which you please, and in the name of the Lord Jesus Christ it shall be done."

"That is not the kind of miracle I want," said the preacher.

"Then, sir," replied Joseph, "I can perform none, I am not going to bring any trouble upon anybody else, sir, to convince you. I will tell you what you make me think of—the very first person who asked a sign of the Savior, for it is written, in the New Testament, that Satan came to the Savior in the desert, when he was hungry with forty days' fasting, and said, 'If you be the Son of God, command these stones to be made bread.' And now," said Joseph, "the children of the devil and his servants have been asking for signs ever since; for signs to prove the truth of the gospel which He preached. The Savior replied, 'It is a wicked and an adulterous generation that seeketh a sign,' etc."

But the poor preacher had so much faith in the power of the Prophet that he daren't risk being struck blind, lame, dumb, or having one hand withered, or anything of the kind. We have frequently heard men calling for signs without knowing actually what they did want. Could he not have tested the principles, and thus have ascertained the truth? But this is not the disposition of men of the religious world.[10]

Zacharias obviously wasn't asking for a sign in the same sense as this preacher. But he had doubted a promise from the Lord and had hesitated to exercise his faith in the message of an arch-angel, second only to Adam in authority.

Zacharias was so long in the temple that everyone marveled. When he came out they realized that something significant had taken place.

> *And the people waited for Zacharias, and marveled that he tarried so long in the temple. And when he came out, he could not speak unto them; and they perceived that he had seen a vision in the temple; for he beckoned unto them, and remained speechless.*
>
> *And as soon as the days of his ministration were accomplished, he departed to his own house.*
>
> *And after those days, his wife Elizabeth conceived, and hid herself five months, saying, Thus hath the Lord dealt with me in the days wherein he looked on me, to take away my reproach from among men.* (JST, Luke 1:21–25)

Notes

1. LDS Bible Dictionary, s.v. "Herod," 700–701.
2. As quoted by Paul Smith, "The Birth of the Messiah," an unpublished script for a slide presentation, Dec. 1984.
3. LDS Bible Dictionary, s.v. "Herod," 700–701.
4. James E. Talmage, *Jesus the Christ* (Salt Lake City: Deseret Book, 1977), 97–98.
5. Bruce R. McConkie, *The Mortal Messiah*, 4 vols. (Salt Lake City: Deseret Book, 1979), 1:303–4.
6. Ibid., 305.
7. See LDS Bible Dictionary, s.v. "Nazarite," 737.
8. Joseph Smith, *Teachings of the Prophet Joseph Smith*, sel. Joseph Fielding Smith (Salt Lake City: Deseret Book, 1976], 157.
9. Bruce R. McConkie, *The Mortal Messiah*, 1:311–12, footnote 5.
10. George A. Smith, in *Journal of Discourses*, Volume 2:326–327. Address delivered 24 June 1855 in the Salt Lake Tabernacle.

EIGHT

The Glorious Announcement to Mary

I T HAD BEEN AT LEAST half a year since Gabriel had visited Zacharias and revealed the miraculous birth Elizabeth would experience. John the Baptist, Jesus' second cousin, the forerunner called to prepare the way, would be six months older than the Messiah.

> And in the sixth month the angel Gabriel was sent from God, unto a city of Galilee, named Nazareth.
>
> To a virgin, espoused to a man whose name was Joseph, of the house of David; and the virgin's name was Mary.
>
> And the angel came in unto her and said, Hail, thou virgin, who art highly favored of the Lord. The Lord is with thee, for thou art chosen and blessed among women.
>
> And when she saw the angel, she was troubled at his saying, and pondered in her mind what manner of salutation this should be.
>
> And the angel said unto her, Fear not, Mary, for thou hast found favor with God.
>
> And behold, thou shalt conceive, and bring forth a son, and shall call his name Jesus. (JST, Luke 1:26–31)

Both Mary and Joseph were commanded by revelation to name the child Jesus. The name in Aramaic is *Yeshua* (the Greek transliteration is *Joshua*) and means "Savior" or "Deliverer." As a child he would be known as *Joshua bar Joseph*, Joshua the son of Joseph the Carpenter. But the angel who visited Mary declared his real paternity:

He shall be great, and shall be called the Son of the Highest; and the Lord God shall give unto him the throne of his father David. (JST, Luke 1:32).

Some mistakenly assume from other scriptures that Jesus was the son of the Holy Ghost (see Matthew 1:20; Luke 1:35). Jesus was the "Son of the Highest, and 'the Highest' is the first member of the godhead, not the third."[1] (See Luke 1:28–35; 1 Nephi 11:18–20; and Alma 7:10.)

The First Presidency (Joseph F. Smith, Anthon H. Lund, and Charles W. Penrose) issued a Christmas message in 1914 that included this testimony: "We bow to Him as the veritable Son of the living God in the fullest sense of the hallowed term. As Mary was His saintly mother, so the Mighty God was His everlasting and literal Father."[2]

Jesus Christ is literally the Son of God the Father,[3] but sometimes in the scriptures He is referred to as the "Son of Man," and a few have mistakenly assumed that He was the son of Joseph the Carpenter. In a revelation received in December 1830, Joseph Smith learned that "in the language of Adam, Man of Holiness is [Heavenly Father's] name, and the name of his Only Begotten is the Son of Man, even Jesus Christ" (Moses 6:57). The Eternal Father is a "Man of Holiness"—a Holy Man, a resurrected and divinely empowered God, who is omniscient, omnipresent, and omnicaring![4]

Christ's birth is the most unique of any on earth. It was "a miracle," Elder Melvin J. Ballard explained, "such as the world had never known— not a miracle in the sense of happening contrary to nature's law, nevertheless a miracle through the operation of a higher law, such as the human mind ordinarily fails to comprehend or regard as possible."[5] Because He was begotten of Elohim, the Eternal Father, and born of a mortal mother, Mary, "not in violation of natural law but in accordance with a higher manifestation of it," His nature would have the combined powers of Godhood with the capacity and possibility of mortality. No one else but the Eternal Father was capable or worthy to be the Savior's father.

His divine birth is directly related to His power to perform the Atonement (see Alma 34:10–14). Because Jesus was born of Mary, He inherited the capacity to die. Because Jesus is the Only Begotten Son of the Father in the flesh, He inherited the power of immortality, the power to live indefinitely, which enabled Him to suffer more than man could suffer (Mosiah 3:7–8), including the capability to suffer the pains of all mankind and to break the bands of death (John 5:26). He was the only being who had the power to lay down His life and to take it up again. He overcame death and atoned for sin, that we might have the ability to be resurrected and inherit eternal life (see Alma 34:10–14).

As Elder James E. Talmage further explained, "In His nature would be combined the powers of Godhood with the capacity and possibilities of mortality; and . . . through the ordinary operation of the fundamental law of heredity declared of God, demonstrated by science, and admitted by philosophy . . . the Child Jesus was to inherit the physical, mental and spiritual traits, tendencies, and powers that characterized His parents: one immortal and glorified—God, the other human—woman."[6]

Many people in the Christian world today want to believe in Jesus, but only as a great human being, a terrific individual—not of divine origin. They feel uncomfortable about the concept of the miraculous virgin birth. Others have assumed that Mary was the one who experienced a "divine birth" or an "immaculate conception." They reason that if Jesus was divine, His mother could not have been mortal. And because the biblical accounts say so little about what happened in Gethsemane, some are confused about the important role Gethsemane played in Christ's atoning sacrifice. Although the scriptures resolutely declare that Jesus Christ rose from the tomb with a glorified body of flesh and bone (Luke 24:39–40), few Christian denominations today, if any, believe in a literal, physical resurrection. Thus, if Christ's divine birth is denied, all of the Atonement must be rejected as well. One could not have been accomplished without the other. It was the dual inheritance that came from a mortal mother and a divine Father that made the Atonement even possible.

For example, if Jesus had been born of two mortal parents, then He could not have had the power to overcome death. He could not have endured the infinite pain and suffering of Gethsemane.[7] He undoubtedly would have sinned and thus, like all other mortals, would have been under the demands of the law of justice.

If, however, Jesus had been born of two divine parents, then He would not have died; He would have been immortal. He would have been impervious to physical pain and suffering and so would not have been able to experience any pain and agony in the Garden. He would not have been subject to the temptation and the opportunity to sin. He could, therefore, never understand us or the pain we go through when we make mistakes.

But because He was born of a divine parent and a mortal parent, He inherited the power to die as well as rise again. None of Joseph and

Mary's children could have done that. Christ had capability to suffer like mortals but could endure much more than any person ever could (D&C 19:15–19; Mosiah 3:7). The sons and daughters of Joseph and Mary could not do that.

The angel Gabriel continued his glorious announcement to Mary:

> *And the Lord God shall give unto him the throne of his father David; and he shall reign over the house of Jacob forever; and of his kingdom there shall be no end.* (JST, Luke 1:33)

David was one of the most powerful and influential kings Israel ever produced. He reigned ten centuries before Christ, and still Matthew paid tribute to Christ by calling Him "the Son of David" (Matthew 1:1). Christ's birth into this royal line fulfilled prophecy (see 2 Samuel 7:11–14). King David's reign over Israel came at a time when Israel was at the height of glory. David's reign was a type of Christ's future reign. Many of the prophets had foretold of a "new David" who would be raised up and rule in Israel as King David once had done.[8] The Jewish people at the time of Christ were anxiously looking for the Deliverer who would free them from the political bondage of Rome. They misunderstood the prophetic passages referring to the salvation Christ would bring to Israel at His Second Coming, when Christ's Kingdom will be established throughout the earth and when He will reign personally as Lord of lords and King of kings. And in a broader sense, they misunderstood the greater freedom this new eternal "David" offers—freedom from the spiritual bondage of death and hell.

It's interesting that Jews still look for this new David. They pilgrimage to King David's tomb just outside the wall of the old city of Jerusalem and weep and pray for the second David to come. Many of them name one of their sons David, hoping that he'll be the one to fulfill the prophecies. Latter-day revelation helps us understand how these prophecies have already been fulfilled. The second David is Christ. He will come and save Israel, both physically and spiritually.

This announcement must have startled Mary in a way that we can scarcely imagine. Of all the women on earth she would bear the Only Begotten Son of God the Eternal Father in the flesh, the descendant of King David who would reign in peace over all the earth. This meant that Mary's son was to be the long awaited Messiah. Quite an announcement to such a young woman—to any woman! Mary wondered how the angel's wonderful announcement would be fulfilled because she was not married and therefore could not have children.

Then said Mary unto the angel; How can this be? (JST, Luke 1:34)

In answer to her question, Gabriel then reverently explained how this miraculous conception would take place. "

And the angel answered and said unto her, The Holy Ghost shall come upon thee, and the power of the Highest shall overshadow thee. Therefore also, that holy child that shall be born of thee shall be called the Son of God. (JST, Luke 1:33–35)

The angel's explanation to Mary is probably the clearest explanation of the fatherhood of God and the divine Sonship of Christ in the scriptures. The specific details of this unparalleled event have been reverently passed over in the scriptural accounts, yet the testimonies borne by prophets leave no doubt as to its reality.[9] The prophet Alma learned by revelation of the sacred gestation: "But behold, the Spirit hath said this much unto me . . . the Son of God cometh upon the face of the earth. And behold, he shall be born of Mary, at Jerusalem which is the land of our forefathers [Jesus was born "at" the land or province of Jerusalem, "in" the city of Bethlehem which is just six miles from the city of Jerusalem itself], she being a virgin, a precious and chosen vessel, who shall be overshadowed and conceive by the power of the Holy Ghost, and bring forth a son, yea, even the Son of God" (Alma 7:12).

The prophet Nephi similarly testified of this sacred birth: "I looked and beheld the great city of Jerusalem, and also other cities. And I behold the city of Nazareth; and in the city of Nazareth I beheld a virgin, and she was exceedingly fair and white [pure]. And it came to pass that I saw the heavens open; and an angel came down and stood before me; and he said unto me: Nephi, what beholdest thou? And I said unto him: A virgin, most beautiful and fair above all other virgins. Behold, the virgin whom thou seest is the mother of the Son of God, after the manner of the flesh" (1 Nephi 11:13–15, 18).

Elder McConkie likewise testified of the foreordained role Mary had in this divine drama:

Can we speak too highly of her whom the Lord has blessed above all women? There was only one Christ, and there is only one Mary. Each was noble and great in the pre-existence, and each was foreordained to the ministry he or she performed. We cannot but think that the Father would choose the greatest female spirit to be the mother of his Son, even as he chose the male spirit like unto him to be the Savior. This is not to say that we should give any heed or credence to the false doctrines that say that Mary has been assumed bodily into heaven, that she is an intercessor who hears prayers and pleads with her Son on behalf of those who pray to her; or that she should be esteemed as co-redemptrix with the Redeemer—all of which are part of a great system of worship that did not originate in the courts on high. As our spirits recoil from these perversions of true religion, we should nonetheless maintain a balanced view and hold up Mary with that proper high esteem which is hers.[10]

After hearing the angel Gabriel's announcement, Mary was understandably awestruck. Who would have believed her story if she were to tell them? Elder McConkie observed that her story would not have been "believed any more than was Joseph Smith's when he—about the same age as Mary was at the time—announced that the Father and the Son had visited him to usher in a new gospel dispensation. Visions and revelations (to the carnally minded) were things of the past; everyone knew that!"[11]

But there was at least one whose heart would understand how Mary felt. Gabriel told Mary to go to Elizabeth, her cousin, and to trust in the Lord because all things would occur just as he had said.

> *And behold, thy cousin Elizabeth, she hath also conceived a son in her old age; and this is the sixth month with her who is called barren. For with God nothing shall be impossible.* (JST, Luke 1:36–37)

Rather than seek for a sure sign (as Zacharias had) that these things would be, Mary submitted humbly to do whatsoever she was asked.

> *And Mary said, Behold the handmaid of the Lord; be it unto me according to thy word. And the angel departed from her.* (JST, Luke 1:36–38)

"THIS IS MY BELOVED SON"

There are two different genealogies for the Savior in the four Gospels (see Matthew 1:1–17; Luke 3:23–28). Joseph and Mary were cousins and were both descendants of King David. Jesus literally was the heir to the throne. He truly was the King of the Jews. As Elder James E. Talmage explained, "Had Judah been a free and independent nation, ruled by her rightful sovereign, Joseph the carpenter would have been her crowned king; and his lawful successor to the throne would have been Jesus of Nazareth, the King of the Jews."[12]

There are a few differences between the two genealogies found in the Gospels. "The critics of the Bible," Elder Maxwell counselled, who "complain that the genealogy of Jesus is rendered differently in Matthew 1 and Luke 3 need to ponder the First Vision. The Father introduced Jesus with these words: 'This is my Beloved Son. Hear Him!' What other genealogy is needed?"[13]

Matthew's account of the Savior's pedigree follows the royal successors to David's throne. It is not a strict genealogical father-to-son list because the eldest heir to the throne may have been a grandson, a nephew, or other relative of the reigning monarch. Matthew began with Father Abraham and traced Jesus' genealogy down to Joseph the Carpenter. He wanted the Jewish people to understand the position of Jesus of Nazareth as (1) a Son of Abraham, (2) a Son of King David, and (3) the King of Israel, rightful heir to the throne.

Luke's account, however, is a father-to-son listing from King David to Joseph. Jesus was not Joseph's son, of course, but since Joseph and Mary were cousins, their genealogy was essentially the same as the one listed for Mary (see Luke 3:23–28).

Another major difference between the two genealogies is that four women are named in Matthew's record—Tamar, Rahab, Ruth, and Bathsheba. As Robert L. Millet has written, at least three good explanations have been offered for why these particular women were included:[14]

> First of all, Jerome recognized the four women as sinners and stated that their inclusion in the list foreshadowed the role of the Messiah in saving men and women from sin. Second, Martin Luther recognized that all four women were regarded as foreigners, thus showing that Jesus, the Jewish Messiah, was in fact related by genealogy to the Gentiles. Third, some have recognized that all of these women, like Mary, were involved in an extraordinary or unusual union with their respective partners, unions which seemed scandalous to outsiders but continued the sacred lineage of the Messiah. Each of them represented how God could use the unexpected to triumph over man-made barriers and eventually bring about the birth of the Christ. Matthew had chosen women who would, in history, typify Mary, the mother of Jesus.[15]

Some may feel that the fact that Christ descended from David and Bathsheba, or from Judah and Tamar, somehow affects His divinity.

Because of God's foreknowledge, He could have seen to it that Christ was born through pure and undefiled lines, but He chose not to and as Joseph Smith said, "Whatever God requires [or does] is right, no matter what it is."[16]

His ancestors' transgressions did not prevent Christ from coming through their lineage. Christ was not responsible for their wrongdoings. They were. In every family there are those who transgress the laws of God. Perhaps this helps us understand that we don't need to worry about what our ancestors did but concern ourselves with our own righteousness. Besides, some of the greatest mortals who have ever lived have come from broken homes (like Moses), had idolatrous parents (like Abraham), or were adopted by relatives (like Esther). We should remember, regardless of what our mortal ancestry is like, our spiritual pedigree chart is only one line long: "I am a child of God."

Ponder what these few verses of genealogy in Matthew chapter 1 and Luke chapter 3 really mean to us as mortals and to Jesus, the Great Jehovah made flesh. The Great I Am, the Firstborn of the Father in the premortal existence who attained the status of Godhood while there, was willing to not only come to earth but to sacrifice all of the power and honor He held and place His life on the altar for us. Gerald N. Lund helps us appreciate why these genealogies of Jesus are significant:

> As we read the scriptures that prophesied the coming of Christ into the world, we sense that the ancients had a different perspective on this event than perhaps we in the latter days do. This difference probably stems from the fact that, to them, Jehovah was their God. He was the God with whom they dealt. He was the Lord of all the earth. He was the Almighty, the Lord of Hosts. They viewed Jehovah in a way similar to the way we view God the Father. In the latter days, we start with a view of Jesus in his mortal ministry and think of him secondarily as Jehovah, but to them he was not yet come in the flesh, and so the idea that their God—this almighty, all-powerful, all-knowing being—would come down to earth, take upon himself a body of flesh, and be born of woman left them with a great sense of awe and wonder.[17]

Consider what Jesus was before He left His Father to inhabit His mortal body. He was the Creator. He could speak, and the elements would obey to form worlds, solar systems, and galaxies. He had already created innumerable worlds (Moses 1:32, 35). The power of His Spirit is everywhere present. It fills the earth, sun, moon and stars and by virtue of the spiritual energy emanating from Him, all things have life and power (see D&C 88:7–13). He was Jehovah, God of the Old Testament. He held stature and power, and we gladly chose to follow his magnificent example.[18]

Paul taught the Philippians, "Let this mind be in you, which was also in Christ Jesus." (Let Jesus be our model of humility and submission.)

"Who, being in the form of God" (meaning that He became like God, His Father; see Moses 1:32–35 and D&C 88:7–13);

"Thought it not robbery to be equal with God." (The Greek word translated as "robbery" means something that one refuses to give up.)

"But made himself of no reputation" (The Greek phrase used here means "emptied himself," or in other words, he divested himself of the glory, power, and position that he had held before);

"And took upon him the form of a servant, and was made in the likeness of man." (He entered the tiny, fragile body of an infant, a body subject to pain, to physical needs, to ridicule, to crucifixion.)

"And being found in fashion as a man, he humbled himself, and became obedient unto death, even the death of the cross." (The Greek word *schemata*, or *fashion*, means "the outward person only." The thought expressed here is that although the outward man was like all other men, the inward man, who did not prize his premortal stature and position so much that he would seize it and refuse to let it go, was willing to go to the cross to work out the plan for our salvation by submitting to the Father's will.)

This powerful being is He whom we worship. As we read the scriptures about His genealogy and birth, it helps to remember who He was and what He consented to do for us. May we share our own witness of Him with our families and joy in the purpose for His coming to our earth.

Notes

1. Bruce R. McConkie, *Doctrinal New Testament Commentary*, 3 vols. (Salt Lake City, Utah: Bookcraft, 1965–1973), 1:83.

2. James R. Clark, comp., *Messages of the First Presidency of The Church of Jesus Christ of Latter-day Saints*, 6 vols. (Salt Lake City: Bookcraft, 1965–75], 4:319; emphasis added.

3. The Gospel of John is filled with testimony of the Divine Sonship of Christ. He is the Only Begotten of the Father in the flesh

(see John 1:14), and *begotten* is a word clearly understood in the ordinary sense. "Only Begotten" is the translation of the Greek *monogenes,* from the roots monos, "only," and genes, "born."

"For the Father himself loveth," Jesus told his Apostles, "because ye have loved me, and have believed that I came out from God. I came forth from the Father." The Apostles understood this to be a literal statement and replied, "Lo, now speakest thou plainly, and speakest no proverb" (John 16:27–29).

Nephi declares a similar testimony. He wrote that Jesus was born "the Son of God, after the manner of the flesh" (1 Nephi 11:18).

4. The Prophet Joseph Smith taught: "God himself was once as we are now, and is an exalted man, and sits enthroned in yonder heavens! That is the great secret. If the veil were rent today, and the great God who holds this world in orbit, and who upholds all worlds and all things by his power, was to make himself visible,—I say, if you were to see him today, you would see him like a man in form—like yourselves in all the person, image, and very form as a man; for Adam was created in the very fashion, image and likeness of God, and received instruction from, and walked, talked and conversed with him, as one man talks and communes with another.

"... It is the first principle of the Gospel to know for a certainty the Character of God, and to know that we may converse with him as one man converses with another, and that he was once like us; yea, that God himself, the Father of us all, dwelt on an earth, the same as Jesus Christ himself did. ...

"Here, then, is eternal life—to know the only wise and true God; and you have got to learn how to be Gods yourselves, and to be kings and priests to God, the same as all Gods have done before you, namely, by going from one small degree to another, and from a small capacity to a great one; from grace to grace, from exaltation to exaltation, until you attain to the resurrection of the dead, and are able to dwell in everlasting burnings, and to sit in glory, as do those who sit enthroned in everlasting power" (Joseph Smith, *Teachings of the Prophet Joseph Smith,* sel. Joseph Fielding Smith [Salt Lake City, Utah: Deseret Book, 1976], 345–47).

5. Melvin J. Ballard, *Sermons and Missionary Services of Melvin J. Ballard,* 166.

6. James E. Talmage, *Jesus the Christ* (Salt Lake City: Deseret Book, 1977), 81.

7. James E. Talmage commented, "Christ's agony in the garden is unfathomable by the finite mind, both as to intensity and cause. ...

"He struggled and groaned under a burden such as no other being who has lived on earth might even conceive as possible. It was not physical pain, nor mental anguish alone, that caused Him to suffer such torture as to produce an extrusion of blood from every pore; but a spiritual agony of soul such as only God was capable of experiencing. No other man, however great his powers of physical or mental endurance, could have suffered so; for his human organism would have succumbed, and syncope would have produced unconsciousness and welcome oblivion. In that hour of anguish Christ met and overcame all the horrors that Satan, 'the prince of this world' could inflict. . . .

"In some manner, actual and terribly real though to man incomprehensible, the Savior took upon Himself the burden of the sins of mankind from Adam to the end of the world. Modern revelation assists us to a partial understanding of the awful experience. In March 1830, the glorified Lord, Jesus Christ, thus spake: 'For behold, I, God, have suffered these things for all, that they might not suffer if they would repent, but if they would not repent, they must suffer even as I, which suffering caused myself, even God, the greatest of all, to tremble because of pain, and to bleed at every pore, and to suffer both body and spirit: and would that I might not drink the bitter cup and shrink—nevertheless, glory be to the Father, and I partook and finished my preparations unto the children of men' (D&C 19:16–19).

"From the terrible conflict in Gethsemane, Christ emerged a victor. Though in the dark tribulation of that fearful hour He had pleaded that the bitter cup be removed from His lips, the request, however oft repeated, was always conditional; the accomplishment of the Father's will was never lost sight of as the object of the Son's supreme desire. The further tragedy of the night, and the cruel inflictions that awaited Him on the morrow, to culminate in the frightful tortures of the cross, could not exceed the bitter anguish through which He had successfully passed (*Jesus the Christ*, 613–614).

8. See Jeremiah 23:5–6; 30:8–9; Ezekiel 34:22–31; and Bruce R. McConkie, *Promised Messiah*, (Salt Lake City: Deseret Book, 1978), 192–95.

9. See *The Growing Edge*, Church Educational System newsletter, vol. 14 (December 1981).

10. Bruce R. McConkie, *The Mortal Messiah*, 4 vols. (Salt Lake City, Utah: Deseret Book, 1979), 1:326, footnote 4.

11. Ibid., 327, footnote 5.

12. James E. Talmage, *Jesus the Christ*, 87.

13. Neal A. Maxwell, *We Talk of Christ, We Preach of Christ* (Salt Lake City: Deseret Book, 1984), 169.

14. See Raymond E. Brown, *The Birth of the Messiah* (New York: Doubleday and Co., 1977), 71–74.

15. Robert L. Millet, "The Birth of the Messiah: A Closer Look at the Infancy Narrative of Matthew," in *A Symposium on the New Testament* (Salt Lake City: The Church of Jesus Christ of Latter-day Saints, 1980), 138–39.

16. Joseph Smith, *Teachings*, 256.

17. Gerald N. Lund, "Knowest Thou the Condescension of God?" *Doctrines of the Book of Mormon: The 1991 Sperry Symposium* (Salt Lake City: Deseret Book, 1992), 81.

18. *The Growing Edge*, Church Educational System newsletter, vol. 14 (Dec. 1981).

NINE

The Birth of John the Baptist

EVENTS IN AMERICA THE YEAR BEFORE CHRIST WAS BORN

The prophesied signs began to appear, but the unbelievers said that it was not "reasonable" to believe in Christ or in His coming to Jerusalem. Marginal members will always be swallowed up in the secular swamps of pride and the philosophies of psycho-ceramics (cracked pots that can hold no water! See Jeremiah 2:13).

> But it came to pass in the ninetieth year of the reign of the judges, there were great signs given unto the people, and wonders; and the words of the prophets began to be fulfilled. And angels did appear unto men, wise men, and did declare unto them glad tidings of great joy; thus in this year the scriptures began to be fulfilled.
>
> Nevertheless, the people began to harden their hearts, all save it were the most believing part of them, both of the Nephites and also of the Lamanites, and began to depend upon their own strength and upon their own wisdom, saying: Some things they may have guessed right, among so many; but behold, we know that all these great and marvelous works cannot come to pass, of which has been spoken.
>
> And they began to reason and to contend among themselves, saying: That it is not reasonable that such a being as a Christ shall come; if so, and he be the Son of God, the Father of heaven and of earth, as it has been spoken, why will he not show himself unto us as well as unto them who shall be at Jerusalem? Yea, why will he not show himself in this land as well as in the land of Jerusalem? But behold, we know that this is a

wicked tradition, which has been handed down unto us by our fathers, to cause us that we should believe in some great and marvelous thing which should come to pass, but not among us, but in a land which is far distant, a land which we know not; therefore they can keep us in ignorance, for we cannot witness with our own eyes that they are true. And they will, by the cunning and the mysterious arts of the evil one, work some great mystery which we cannot understand, which will keep us down to be servants to their words, and also servants unto them, for we depend upon them to teach us the word; and thus will they keep us in ignorance if we will yield ourselves unto them, all the days of our lives.

And many more things did the people imagine up in their hearts, which were foolish and vain; and they were much disturbed, for Satan did stir them up to do iniquity continually; yea, he did go about spreading rumors and contentions upon all the face of the land, that he might harden the hearts of the people against that which was good and against that which should come.

And notwithstanding the signs and the wonders which were wrought among the people of the Lord, and the many miracles which they did, Satan did get great hold upon the hearts of the people upon all the face of the land. (Helaman 16:13–23)

MARY VISITS ELIZABETH

And in those days, Mary went into the hill country with haste, into a city of Juda; And entered into the house of Zacharias, and saluted Elizabeth. (JST, Luke 1:39–40)

These two women, related by blood, were also related now by the mission each was called to perform. Elizabeth would bear the great prophet who would prepare the way, and Mary would bear the Son of God, the prophesied Messiah of all mankind.

And it came to pass, that when Elizabeth heard the salutation of Mary, the babe leaped in her womb. (JST, Luke 1:41)

This is no ordinary leap. Even before he was born, John began to bear witness of Christ. Joseph Smith was told that John the Baptist was that very prophet "whom God raised up, being filled with the Holy Ghost from his mother's womb" (D&C 84:27). Elder McConkie commented that "from the scriptural accounts it is clear that this means, not alone from the time he came forth out of the womb, but from the time that he as a conscious identity, the spirit having entered the body, was yet encased therein,"[1] John received the Holy Ghost and began testifying of Christ.

In addition to John's recognition of Mary, the mother of Jesus, Elizabeth also receive a testimony at that moment. She was filled with the spirit of prophecy:

> *And Elizabeth was filled with the Holy Ghost, and she spake out with a loud voice and said, Blessed art thou among women, and blessed is the fruit of thy womb.*
>
> *And why is it, that this blessing is upon me, that the mother of my Lord should come to me? For lo, as soon as the voice of thy salutation sounded in mine ears, the babe leaped in my womb for joy.*
>
> *And blessed art thou who believed, for those things which were told thee by the angel of the Lord, shall be fulfilled.* (JST, Luke 1:41–43)

Mary was also filled with the Holy Ghost:

> *And Mary said, My soul doth magnify the Lord,*
>
> *And my spirit rejoiceth in God my Savior. For he hath regarded the low estate of his handmaiden; for behold, from henceforth all generations shall call me blessed.*
>
> *For he who is mighty hath done to me great things; and I will magnify his holy name,*
>
> *For his mercy on those who fear him from generation to generation.*
>
> *He hath showed strength with his arm; he hath scattered the proud in the imagination of their hearts.*
>
> *He hath put down the mighty from their seats; and exalted them of low degree.*
>
> *He hath filled the hungry with good things; but the rich he hath sent empty away.*
>
> *He hath helped his servant Israel in remembrance of his mercy,*
>
> *As he spake to our fathers, to Abraham, and to his seed forever.*
>
> *And Mary abode with Elizabeth about three months.* (JST, Luke 1:44–55)

THE MIRACULOUS BIRTH OF JOHN THE BAPTIST

> *Now Elizabeth's full time came that she should be delivered; and she brought forth a son.*
>
> *And her neighbors, and her cousins heard how the Lord had showed great mercy upon her; and they rejoiced with her.*
>
> *And it came to pass, that on the eighth day they came to circumcise the child.* (JST, Luke 1:56–58)

In addition to the circumcision, we also know by modern revelation, as mentioned earlier, that some time during this day John was ordained by an "angel of God . . . unto this power, to overthrow the Kingdom of the Jews, and to make straight the way of the Lord" and to prepare his people for "the coming of the Lord" (D&C 84:28).

> *And they called him Zacharias, after the name of his father.*
>
> *And his mother answered and said, Not so; but he shall be called John.*
>
> *And they said unto her, There is none of thy kindred that is called by this name.*
>
> *And they made signs to his father, and asked him how he would have him called.*
>
> *And he asked for a writing table, and wrote, saying, His name is John, and they all marveled. And his mouth was opened immediately, and he spake with his tongue, and praised God.*
>
> *And fear came on all who dwelt round about them. And all these sayings were noised abroad throughout all the hill country of Judea.*
>
> *And all they that heard them laid them up in their hearts, saying, What manner of child shall this be? And the hand of the Lord was with him.* (JST Luke 1:58–65)

ZACHARIAS REJOICES AND PROPHETICALLY BLESSES HIS SON

After Zacharias' mouth was opened, he prayerfully thanked the Lord and prophesied, by the power of the Spirit, of the mission of his own son and of the mission of the Son of God:

> *And his father Zacharias was filled with the Holy Ghost, and prophesied, saying,*
>
> *Blessed be the Lord God of Israel; for he hath visited and redeemed his people,*
>
> *And hath raised up an horn of salvation for us, in the house of his servant David,*
>
> *As he spake by the mouth of his holy prophets, ever since the world began,*
>
> *That we should be saved from our enemies, and from the hand of all those who hate us;*
>
> *To perform the mercy promised to our fathers, and to remember his holy covenant;*
>
> *The oath which he sware to our father Abraham,*

That he would grant unto us, that we, being delivered out of the hand of our enemies, might serve him without fear,

In holiness and righteousness before him, all the days of our lives.

And thou, child, shalt be called the prophet of the Highest, for thou shalt go before the face of the Lord to prepare his ways,

To give knowledge of salvation unto his people, by baptism for the remission of their sins,

Through the tender mercy of our God; whereby the dayspring from on high hath visited us,

To give light to them who sit in darkness and the shadow of death; to guide our feet into the way of peace. (JST Luke 1:66–78)

From latter-day revelation, we know also that John "was baptized while he was yet in his childhood" (D&C 84:28).

And the child grew, and waxed strong in spirit, and was in the deserts until the day of his showing unto Israel. (JST, Luke 1:79)

There was a reason for John's being raised in the wilderness of the deserts. His life was spared when Herod's edict was given to slaughter all the young children.[2] Zacharias was put to death by Herod's soldiers for refusing to disclose where his wife, Elizabeth, and their young son, John, had fled for safety.

MARY'S DEPARTURE

And Mary . . . returned to her own house. (Luke 1:56)

Notes

1. Bruce R. McConkie, *The Mortal Messiah*, 4 vols. (Salt Lake City: Deseret Book, 1979), 1:327, footnote 6.

2. See Joseph Smith, *Teachings of the Prophet Joseph Smith* (Salt Lake City: Deseret Book, 1976), 261.

TEN

THE DAYS WERE ACCOMPLISHED

That She Should Be Delivered

THE ANNUNCIATION TO JOSEPH

When unexpected and unforeseen events come into our lives, they are often difficult to deal with. Catching us by surprise, they can throw us off track. Joseph's life took such an unanticipated turn as he learned of Mary's condition. "So often we think of the Christmas story from Mary's perspective—what she must have thought and how she felt. Suppose Joseph had kept a journal during those months. What insights could he have given us? What might have been his response to those events?"[1]

Matthew recorded a portion of the struggles and decisions Joseph was facing:

> *Now, as it is written, the birth of Jesus Christ was on this wise. After his mother, Mary, was espoused to Joseph, before they came together, she was found with child of the Holy Ghost.* (JST, Matthew 2:1)

Mary was *espoused* to Joseph. They were not married but were promised to each other under the strictest social mores. According to ancient Jewish laws and customs, marriage was a two-step process. First, a young couple became betrothed (espoused). Second, several months or even a year later the more formal wedding took place and the young couple was officially married. In a sense, becoming betrothed or espoused was like becoming engaged in our society today, only it carried the fullest weight of social responsibility. In fact, it was legally binding. Even though the espoused couple could not yet live together, they were legally committed to and reserved for each other and were referred to as husband and wife.[2]

Under the law, their relationship could only be broken by death or by legal separation similar to a divorce. Since Mary was virtually regarded as the wife of Joseph, unfaithfulness on her part during their engagement was punishable by death (see Deuteronomy 22:23–24). Imagine the heartbreak and chagrin of Joseph when he discovered that his betrothed wife was expecting a child. Joseph had two alternatives: first, demand that Mary submit to a public trial and judgment, which, even at this time in Jewish history, may have resulted in Mary's being stoned to death; or second, get a private divorce and sever the espousal contract before witnesses.

> *Then Joseph, her husband, being a just man, and not willing to make her a public example, was minded to put her away privily.* (JST, Matthew 2:2)

Joseph's decision is an obvious witness to his character. He still loved Mary and did not want to subject her to public ridicule and scorn. He did not react with bitterness or spite. "In his agony and uncertainty," Joseph determined to give her a "letter of divorce in the presence of two witnesses rather than make it a matter of public knowledge and possible gossip."[3] We are left to wonder how Joseph must have pondered and prayed, how his faith was tested. It could be that the Lord designed these circumstances to test Joseph and prove him (see Mosiah 23:21). But one thing is for certain—he was merciful to Mary, as Elder Talmage has described: "Joseph was a just man, a strict observer of the law, yet no harsh extremist; moreover he loved Mary and would save her all unnecessary humiliation, whatever might be his own sorrow and suffering. For Mary's sake he dreaded the thought of publicity and therefore determined to have the espousal annulled with such privacy as the law allowed."[4]

The word *just* used to describe him comes from the Greek word *diakos*, which means "to be in conformance to law, or to be righteous." "In Hebrew the word *tzadik* has the same connotation. For example, Melchizedek's name is a title meaning *king* (melchis) *of righteousness* (tzadik). Noah was also called a 'just man and perfect' (Genesis 6:9). The word *just* is often used to describe the attributes of God (see, for example, Deuteronomy 32:4; Isaiah 45:21; Zephaniah 3:5; Acts 3:14). Thus to say that Joseph was a *just* man says a great deal about the man the Father chose to help raise his Son."[5]

Not until after Joseph made his decision did the angel visit him and direct that he should proceed to take Mary as his wife.

> *But while he thought on these things, behold, the angel of the Lord appeared unto him in a vision, saying, Joseph, thou son of David, fear not to take unto thee Mary thy wife; for that which is conceived in her, is of the Holy Ghost. And she shall bring forth a son, and thou shalt call his name Jesus; for he shall save his people from their sins.* (JST, Matthew 2:3–4).

How welcome these words must have been to Joseph! Now he knew there was no doubt about Mary's integrity and purity. Mary's high station was known long before she was born, and Joseph no doubt was also foreordained to the honored place he held. The Prophet Joseph Smith taught that "every man who has a calling to minister to the inhabitants of the world was ordained to that very purpose in the Grand Council of heaven before this world was."[6] Surely Joseph was among the "noble and great ones" who was "chosen before he was born" to have the singular honor of coming to earth as the legal guardian of the Son of the Eternal Father in the flesh (see Abraham 3:22–23). What trust the Father had in him!

Like Joseph of old, we too must cope with unexpected events in our lives. "When they occur and our faith is tested, it would be well for us to exhibit the courage, persistence, and valiance of Joseph. With such faith and determination we, too, can do all that God expects of us and conquer the unexpected problems of life."[7]

> *Now this took place, that all things might be fulfilled, which were spoken of the Lord, by the prophets, saying,*
>
> *Behold, a virgin shall be with child, and shall bring forth a son, and they shall call his name Emmanuel, (which, being interpreted, is, God with us).*
>
> *Then Joseph, awaking out of his vision, did as the angel of the Lord had bidden him, and took unto him his wife;*
>
> *And knew her not until she had brought forth her firstborn son; and they called his name Jesus.* (JST, Matthew 2:5–8)

Jesus is the anglicized form of the Greek word pronounced "Hee-ay-sous." In Hebrew the word was *Yehoshua*, or *Yeshua*, which is usually written as Joshua in English. The word comes from the Hebrew *yasha*, which means "he saved, delivered, or made safe." Thus, as discussed earlier, *Jesus* literally means Savior, a name appropriate for his divine role.

THE DECREE TO BE TAXED

> *And it came to pass in those days, that there went out a decree from Caesar Augustus, that all his empire should be taxed.*
> *This same taxing was when Cyrenius was governor of Syria. And all went to be taxed, everyone in his own city.* (JST, Luke 2:1–3)

The Greek text describes this taxing as actually being more of a registration or census than a tax. "The taxing herein referred to," Elder Talmage affirmed, "may properly be understood as an enrollment, or a registration, whereby a census of Roman subjects would be secured, upon which as a basis the taxation of the different peoples would be determined. This particular census was the second of three such general registrations recorded by historians as occurring at intervals of about twenty years. Had the census been taken by the usual Roman method, each person would have been enrolled at the town of his residence; but the Jewish custom, for which the Roman law had respect, necessitated registration at the cities or towns claimed by the respective families as their ancestral homes."[8]

This census registration was held during the week-long Passover, a festival commemorating Israel's freedom from bondage in Egypt. How ironic it must have been to have to enroll their servitude to Rome during this particular holiday celebration.

> *And Joseph also went up from Galilee, out of the city of Nazareth, into Judea, unto the city of David, which is called Bethlehem; (because he was of the house and lineage of David).*
> *To be taxed, with Mary his espoused wife, she being great with child.* (JST, Luke 2:4–5)

The young couple packed their belongings and started on their way. The journey must have been especially difficult for Mary, who was within days of giving birth. But the trek had to be made—and not just for Rome. It had been prophesied that Jesus would be born in Bethlehem (see Matthew 2:4–5; Micah 5:2). Both Mary and Joseph were descendants of David. Bethlehem was their ancestral home. Christ was known by revelation as the "New David" (Jeremiah 23:5–6) and the "root of David" (Revelation 22:16) and He was to be born in the "city of David." Joseph and Mary may have deliberately gone to Bethlehem to fulfill these prophecies, or they may not have even been aware of them, but in either case they were led by God.

They probably were also not aware of the significance of the town's name in relationship to their child. He who is the Bread of Life was born in Bethlehem, the city whose name means "house of bread."[9] Surely they couldn't have known at that time that He would later feed a multitude with five loaves of bread (see Matthew 14:15–21), make bread the symbol of the sacrifice of his body (see John 6:51), and declare Himself to be the "bread of Life" (John 6:35, 48).[10]

Their journey was over dusty roads and winding paths, a distance of almost ninety miles. "Because thieves roamed the trails and attacks by wild beasts were not unfamiliar, Joseph and Mary probably travelled with other families and kinsmen. Springtime probably made the journey a more pleasant experience with the occasional rains which would paint the hillsides with bright red and yellow lilies. As they came near Bethlehem, the hillsides and fields would have been dotted heavily with goat-skin tents of other weary travellers. He who is called 'the Life' was born in the Springtime when all life is renewed and regenerated."[11]

And so it was, that while they were there, the days were accomplished that she should be delivered. (JST, Luke 2:4–6)

As we rush about with the multitude of shoppers and the large crowds at Christmastime, we are reminded that Bethlehem, too, was crowded. We would do well to ask ourselves whether we are one of the "inn" crowd, or among the "stable" few. "During the hurry of the festive occasion of this Christmas season," Elder Howard W. Hunter challenged, "find time to turn your heart to God."[12]

Notes

1. *The Growing Edge*, Church Educational System newsletter, vol. 14 (Dec. 1981).
2. See Alfred Edersheim, *The Life and Times of Jesus the Messiah,* 2 vols. (1883; reprint, New York: Longmans Green and Co., 1950), 1:354.
3. "Joseph of Nazareth," *LDS Church News* editorial, Dec. 12, 1992, 16.
4. James E. Talmage, *Jesus the Christ,* 84.
5. See *The Growing Edge.*
6. Joseph Smith, *Teachings of the Prophet Joseph Smith,* 365.

7. "Joseph of Nazareth," *LDS Church News* editorial, Dec. 12, 1992, 16.

8. James E. Talmage, *Jesus the Christ*, 91–92.

9. Bethlehem comes from the Aramaic *beth* meaning "house of," and *lechem* meaning "bread." See the *LDS Bible Dictionary*, s.v. "Bethlehem."

10. My thanks to David H. Madsen for tying all these symbols together in his presentation "The Beginning of the Gospels," *A Symposium on the New Testament,* 1984 (Salt Lake City: The Church of Jesus Christ of Latter-day Saints, 1984), 7.

11. See *The Growing Edge*.

12. Howard W. Hunter, "The Real Christmas," in *Speeches of the Year, 1972–1973* (Provo, Utah: Brigham Young University Press, 1973), 69.

ELEVEN

EVENTS IN THE ANCIENT AMERICAS

The Day Before Christ Was Born

THE WICKED HAVE ALWAYS USED every available opportunity to take advantage of the righteous. The meek won't inherit
much on this earth until it becomes the celestial kingdom—then
they get it all! (See Psalm 37:11; Matthew 5:5; 3 Nephi 12:5; D&C 88:17.)
The night before the Savior's birth was no exception:

> *And it came to pass that in the commencement of the ninety and
> second year, behold, the prophecies of the prophets began to be fulfilled
> more fully; for there began to be greater signs and greater miracles wrought
> among the people.*
>
> *But there were some who began to say that the time was past for the
> words to be fulfilled, which were spoken by Samuel, the Lamanite.*
>
> *And they began to rejoice over their brethren, saying: Behold the time
> is past, and the words of Samuel are not fulfilled; therefore, your joy and
> your faith concerning this thing hath been vain.*
>
> *And it came to pass that they did make a great uproar throughout the
> land; and the people who believed began to be very sorrowful, lest by any
> means those things which had been spoken might not come to pass. But
> behold, they did watch steadfastly for that day and that night and that day
> which should be as one day as if there were no night, that they might know
> that their faith had not been vain. (3 Nephi 1:4–8)*

Why were the wicked so glad to see the prophesied signs fail? Why were they not anxiously looking forward to their fulfillment? The answers are too obvious to even discuss. The wicked enjoy their rebellious lifestyle but scare easily when their conscience speaks to them about things as "they really are" (that there is a God) and about "things as they really will be" (that there really is a day of judgement where we will be held accountable for all our words, thoughts, and deeds). "For the Spirit speaketh the truth and lieth not" (Jacob 4:13).

Even Herod, when he heard about the Savior's birth, "feared, yet he believed not the prophets" (JST Matthew 3:4). Cautiously, those whose hearts are conspiring with "evils and designs" (D&C 89:4) take a "wait and see" attitude when their lifestyle is challenged by the whisperings of the Spirit or by the teachings of heaven-sent truth. When it looks like the prophesied day of judgment will not come to pass, they rejoice and celebrate (see 3 Nephi 1:6, above).

It may not be much different in our day just prior to the Second Coming. Commenting on what happened in ancient America, Elder Delbert L. Stapley warned:

> This account of wickedness and contentions among the Nephites prior to the Lord's birth in the meridian of time is duplicated in the wickedness, contentions, and deceptions of our day as we approach the Second Coming of our Lord and Savior, Jesus Christ. Prophecies concerning these days are also being fulfilled and Satan is stirring up the hearts of men to do iniquity continually; and to thwart, if possible, faith in the great event of Christ's Second Coming to earth, which I testify is sure to come to pass. Satan is alert and active. We must be more alert and perceptive of the false and insincere schemes of his agents among us.[1]

> *Now it came to pass that there was a day set apart by the unbelievers, that all those who believed in those traditions should be put to death except the sign should come to pass, which had been given by Samuel the prophet.* (3 Nephi 1:9)

Of all the days in the year the wicked could choose from, why did they pick this particular day? They surely had no clue that that night the sign would be given. Sometimes the Lord inspires the wicked to utter prophecies that they themselves will be judged by. For example, in the Book of Mormon, the inhabitants of Ammonihah told Alma and Amulek that they wouldn't believe their message to repent even if they were to say that the great city of Ammonihah itself would be destroyed in one day. Unfortunately for the people of Ammonihah, that's exactly what the Lord had commanded Alma and Amulek to tell them! (See Alma 9:1–5, 16:9–10.)

Another example occurred at the time of Christ, when Caiaphas, the unworthy high priest, prophesied that "one man should die for the people . . . that the whole nation perish not." Yet, in spite of this prophecy from his own mouth about Christ's sacrifice, Caiaphas took an active part in the attack made upon the Lord and his disciples which resulted in the crucifixion, fulfilling his own prophecy. (See Matthew 26:3, 57; Luke 3:2; John 11:49, 18:13–14, 24, 28; Acts 4:6.)

Man's extremity is God's opportunity. And at the very moment when the lives of all the believers and followers of Christ are being threatened, they were praying for the sign to be given as had been prophesied. Mormon, knowing of our day and needs, carefully recorded what happened among the Nephites:

> Now it came to pass that when Nephi, the son of Nephi, saw this wickedness of his people, his heart was exceedingly sorrowful.
>
> And it came to pass that he went out and bowed himself down upon the earth, and cried mightily to his God in behalf of his people, yea, those who were about to be destroyed because of their faith in the tradition of their fathers.
>
> And it came to pass that he cried mightily unto the Lord, all that day; and behold, the voice of the Lord came unto him, saying:
>
> Lift up your head and be of good cheer; for behold, the time is at hand, and on this night shall the sign be given, and on the morrow come I into the world, to show unto the world that I will fulfill all that which I have caused to be spoken by the mouth of my holy prophets. (3 Nephi 1:10–13)

Christ is the Savior (Luke 2:11) and the Prince of Life (Acts 3:15). It is appropriate that at His birth the lives of those who were facing death for their belief in Him were saved by the sign of His birth. But even greater than physical safety, His coming to earth to work out the Atonement and overcome the effects of the Fall saves all believers from spiritual death (2 Nephi 9:6–10).

> Behold, I come unto my own, to fulfill all things which I have made known unto the children of men from the foundation of the world, and to do the will, both of the Father and of the Son—of the Father because of me, and of the Son because of my flesh. And behold, the time is at hand, and this night shall the sign be given. (3 Nephi 1:14)

Some may wonder how it was possible for the Savior to speak to Nephi the night before his own birth, while he was in Mary's womb. Elder McConkie has written:

> These words, spoken in the name of the Lord Jesus are sometimes used, erroneously, as an argument that the Spirit Christ was not in the body being prepared in Mary's womb, and that therefore the spirit does not enter the body until the moment of birth, when the mother's offspring first breathes the breath of life. This is not true.
>
> As amply attested by the writings of President Brigham Young and others, the spirit enters the body at the time of quickening, whenever that is, and remains in the developing body until the time of birth. In a formal doctrinal statement the First Presidency of the Church (Joseph F. Smith, Anthon H. Lund, and John R. Winder) have said: "The body of man enters upon its career as tiny germ or embryo, which becomes an infant, quickened at a certain stage by the spirit whose tabernacle it is, and the child, after being born, develops into a man." With reference to the words here spoken by the Lord Jesus on the night of his birth, we must understand that someone else, speaking by what is called divine investiture of authority, is speaking the words in the first person as though he were the Lord, when in fact he is only speaking in the Lord's name. In many revelations the Son speaks in this same way as though he were the Father.[2]

Darkness vanishes when the "light of the world" (John 8:12) makes His appearance:

> *And it came to pass that the words which came unto Nephi were fulfilled, according as they had been spoken; for behold, at the going down of the sun there was no darkness; and the people began to be astonished because there was no darkness when the night came.*
>
> *And there were many, who had not believed the words of the prophets, who fell to the earth and became as if they were dead, for they knew that the great plan of destruction which they had laid for those who believed in the words of the prophets had been frustrated; for the sign which had been given was already at hand.* (3 Nephi 1:15–16)

Besides the heavenly lights, another sign of the birth of the eldest son of the "Father of lights" (D&C 67:9) was a new star in the heavens, seen in the old world (Matthew 2:2) and the new (see Helaman 14:5). This incident, and the events which followed, are also similar to the scene which will take place at the Second Coming:

And they began to know that the Son of God must shortly appear; yea, in fine, all the people upon the face of the whole earth from the west to the east, both in the land north and in the land south, were so exceedingly astonished that they fell to the earth.

For they knew that the prophets had testified of these things for many years, and that the sign which had been given was already at hand; and they began to fear because of their iniquity and their unbelief.

And it came to pass that there was no darkness in all that night, but it was as light as though it was mid-day. And it came to pass that the sun did rise in the morning again, according to its proper order; and they knew that it was the day that the Lord should be born, because of the sign which had been given.

And it had come to pass, yea, all things, every whit, according to the words of the prophets.

And it came to pass also that a new star did appear, according to the word. (3 Nephi 1:17–21)

This spectacular solar display will be repeated just prior to His Second Coming. Joseph Smith taught that similar phenomena will take place in the heavens when "the sign of the son of Man" is shown (see Joseph Smith—Matthew 1:33, 36). This sign will be the last great sign shown just before the world sees "the Son of Man coming in the clouds of heaven with power and great glory" (see Joseph Smith—Matthew 1:36). The prophet Zechariah added that at night, when this great light and sign is given, there will be no darkness (Zechariah 14:6–7).[3] The prophet Joseph described how the world will react when they witness the event: "Then will appear one grand sign of the Son of Man in heaven. But what will the world do? They will say it is a planet, a comet, etc. But the Son of Man will come as the sign of the coming of the Son of Man, which will be as the light of the morning cometh out of the east."[4]

Another interesting point to note about the new star that appeared anciently is that it showed up right on time, in the right place, exactly when it was required. That star was created by Christ, and by His power it began to move so it would show up the night it was needed. How many years in advance did Jesus command this star to start moving so that it would show up right on time? Our God is a god of planning![5] Like that star, and with a little planning, you and I can show up right on time in the lives of others, if we'll stay in tune with the Lord's Spirit. Elder Maxwell observed, "The same God that placed that star in a precise orbit millennia before it appeared over Bethlehem in celebration of the birth of the Babe has given at least equal attention to placement of each of us in precise human orbits so that we may, if we will, illuminate the landscape of our individual lives, so that our light may not only lead others but warm them as well."[6]

Not only did this single star bear witness of Him, every star that "rolls upon their wings and in their glory" in the heavens each night bears witness of the Creator. "And any man who hath seen any or the least of these hath seen God moving in his majesty and power" (see D&C 88:41–47). "Sometimes, when talking about his birth as a baby in a manger," President J. Reuben Clark Jr. reminded us, "we forget that he was a god before he was born and that He created this earth and countless others. He was and is a being of great power, glory, and majesty. If you think of this galaxy of ours having within it from the beginning perhaps until now, one million worlds, and multiply that by the number of millions of galaxies, one hundred million galaxies, that surround us, you will then get some view of who this Man we worship is."[7]

But even when the predicted signs undeniably show up, Satan tries to deceive people into rationalizing the truth away.

> *And it came to pass that from this time forth there began to be lyings sent forth among the people, by Satan, to harden their hearts, to the intent that they might not believe in those signs and wonders which they had seen; but notwithstanding these lyings and deceivings the more part of the people did believe, and were converted unto the Lord.*
>
> *And it came to pass that Nephi went forth among the people, and also many others, baptizing unto repentance, in the which there was a great remission of sins. And thus the people began again to have peace in the land.* (3 Nephi 1:22–23)

The significance of the Savior's birth goes almost unnoticed, at least unappreciated, by most of the world. But the impact of that event can bring, in its wake, peace to all those who take note of it. The words to one of our sacred Christmas carols teaches this truth:

O morning stars, together
Proclaim the holy birth,
And praises sing to God the King,
And peace to men on earth.

How silently, how silently
The wondrous gift is giv'n!

So God imparts to human hearts
The blessings of his heav'n.
No ear may hear his coming;
But in this world of sin,
Where meek souls will receive Him, still
The dear Christ enters in.[8]

THE DATE OF HIS BIRTH

What night was this, when the lights and the new star appeared to the Nephites? We celebrate the birth of Christ on December 25. But, as Elder James E. Talmage has written, "It is claimed by many Biblical scholars that December 25, the day celebrated in Christendom as Christmas, cannot be the correct date. We believe April 6th to be the birthday of Jesus Christ as indicated in a revelation of the present dispensation [see D&C 20:1]. . . . This acceptance is admittedly based on faith in modern revelation and in no wise is set forth as the result of chronological research or analysis."[9]

The major reason the world celebrates the birth of Christ on December 25 is that it is the date of the winter solstice, "the time of year when (precisely at midnight, traditionally the hour of Jesus' birth, hence the tradition of the midnight Mass) the days cease becoming dark longer and begin to have more hours of daylight. Thus the forces of light (good) begin to vanquish the forces of darkness (evil). This symbolism was not original with early Christianity but is present in many cultures."[10] Thus, we celebrate Christ's birth in December, at the very time of year we celebrate the rebirth of light—an appropriate symbol and a perfect point in time each year to honor the Savior, the "life and light of the world, your Redeemer, your Lord and your God" (D&C 10:70; Alma 38:9; Mosiah 16:9).

"The exact date is of less consequence than the fact."[11] What matters most is that Christ was born of Mary and is the literal Son of God the Eternal Father.

Notes
1. Delbert L. Stapley, in *Conference Report*, October 1961, 22.
2. Bruce R. McConkie, *Mormon Doctrine*, 2nd ed. (Salt Lake City: Bookcraft, 1966), 17; and *The Mortal Messiah*, 4 vols. (Salt Lake City, Utah: Deseret Book Co., 1979), 1:349.
3. Elder Bruce R. McConkie, *Millennial Messiah* (Salt Lake City: Deseret Book, 1982), 419–20.

4. Joseph Smith, *Teachings of the Prophet Joseph Smith*, 287.

5. See, for example, the heading to D&C 10, where the Lord had prepared for the loss of 116 pages of the Book of Mormon translation centuries before it occurred.

6. Neal A. Maxwell, *That My Family Should Partake* (Salt Lake City: Deseret Book, 1974).

7. J. Reuben Clark Jr., *Behold the Lamb of God* (Salt Lake City: Deseret Book, 1991), 17.

8. Phillips Brooks, "Oh Little Town of Bethlehem," *Hymns*, no. 208.

9. James E. Talmage, *Jesus the Christ*, 104.

President Harold B. Lee once declared, "This is the annual conference of the Church. April 6, 1973, is a particularly significant date because it commemorates not only the anniversary of the organization of the Church of Jesus Christ of Latter-day Saints in this dispensation, but also the anniversary of the birth of the Savior, our Lord and Master, Jesus Christ." President Lee then quoted D&C 20:1 (in *Conference Report*, April 1973, 4).

Charles W. Nibley made this interesting observation about April 6: "A wonderful day, the sixth day of April! Many notable things have occurred on it. The Organization of the Church for one great and notable thing. The Prophet Joseph recites in his own story that it was early in the spring of 1820 . . . when he went into the woods to pray. I like to think of that also as being the sixth day of April. We have no definite knowledge of it, but I believe it in my heart and soul that the sixth day of April was the birthday of the Lord Jesus, our Savior and Redeemer. . . . More likely it was in the spring of the year than on the twenty-fifth day of December, which is celebrated as the birthday of the Savior; yet we go on celebrating that day, and it is all right to do so, inasmuch as that is the day the world generally accepts. But I repeat, it is my individual opinion, firmly fixed in my mind, that the sixth day of April is the birthday of the Savior of the world. I further like to believe that the resurrection of the Redeemer, which marked his triumph over death and the grave, also occurred on the sixth of April, though I have not definite proof" (in *Conference Report*, April 1930, 26–27.)

10. See David H. Madsen, "The Beginning of the Gospels," *A Symposium on the New Testament*, 1984 (Salt Lake City: The Church of Jesus Christ of Latter-day Saints, 1984), 7.

11. Robert J. Matthews, "Christmas and the Birth of Christ," *Instructor Magazine*, 105 (Oct. 1970), 396.

TWELVE

The Birth of the Messiah

I N   O U R   F I R S T   O R   P R E M O R T A L   estate, Jesus was the first spirit child of our Eternal Parents.[1] He grew in grace and power until He stood as one "like unto God" (Abraham 3:24). He sustained the Father's plan, willingly offered himself as the lamb to be slain, the great, required, and last sacrifice, and thus became our Savior and Redeemer. Jesus voluntarily descended from His "throne divine" to walk among men and take upon Himself the trials of mortality. He taught us that whosoever would humble Himself should be exalted (see Matthew 23:12) and He came into the world in the humblest of circumstances.[2] He was foreordained to be the Sacrificial Lamb (John 1:29; 1 Nephi 10:10; Revelation 13:8), and like a lamb, was born in a stable and laid in a manger almost two thousand years ago. The hinge of history swings on the door of that Bethlehem stable.

> *And she brought forth her firstborn son, and wrapped him in swaddling clothes, and laid him in a manger, because there was none to give room for them in the inns.* (JST, Luke 2:7)

There are so many insights packed into this one verse of scripture. This is the greatest moment in earthly history up to that point. The Messiah has come to begin His mission. Our eternal destiny hung on His success. It was the dawn of redeeming grace: "Silent Night! Holy Night! . . . Jesus, Lord at thy birth . . . Jesus, Lord at thy birth."

THE TIME, THE PLACE

"Why did the Father choose to send his Son to earth where and when He did? If that time and place were important, then why did He not send Jesus into the home of the ruling family where He could have had a broad political base of power to work from? Why did He not send the Savior to be born in Enoch's Zion? Think how different His reception would have been there! If the Father had waited until our modern age, the birth could have been reported worldwide via satellite networks. Wouldn't that have been an advantage?"[3]

As the apostle Paul explained in the book of Hebrews, Jesus needed to be exposed to earthly conditions in order to be able to redeem and help us: "Wherefore in all things it behoved him to be made like unto his brethren, that he might be a merciful and faithful high priest in things pertaining to God, to make reconciliation for the sins of the people. For in that he himself hath suffered being tempted [in Greek this word meant tried or subjected to trials], he is able to succor them that are tempted" (Hebrews 2:18).

At a low point in Joseph Smith's life, while languishing in the filth of Liberty Jail, the Lord revealed that He descended below every kind of trying condition we might ever experience. He understands our pain and tried to comfort Joseph with these words: "My son, peace be unto thy soul; thine adversity and afflictions shall be but a small moment. . . . Know thou, my son, that all these things shall give thee experience, and shall be for thy good. The Son of Man hath descended below them all. Art thou greater than he?" (D&C 121:7; 122:7–8).

The phrase "below them all" could refer to each of us individually, or all of us collectively, as well as to all the various conditions of mortality we are subjected to. None of us will ever be able to say to Him, "You don't understand me. No one does." He "comprehends all things," including all things about us because He's been there and beyond (see D&C 88:6–13, 41). After His horrific experience in Gethsemane and on the cross at Calvary, He knew personally every pain, every affliction, every temptation, every sickness, every emotional inadequacy, every infirmity, every weight of sin, and even death (see Alma 7:10–13). He doesn't love us because we're good and do good things. He loves us because He is so good! And He comprehends all things about us (D&C 88:6–13).

Elder Bruce R. McConkie added,

> Could it be that planet earth was chosen as the place for the birth of a God because we on this earth are in greater need for direct and

personal guidance than those who live on other earths? . . .

Joseph made the choice to sleep in the courtyard with the animals, in the stable if you will. And we cannot think other than that there was a divine providence in this. The great God, the Father of us all, intended that his Only Begotten Son should be born in the lowest of circumstances and subject to the most demeaning of surroundings.[4]

"SHE BROUGHT FORTH HER FIRSTBORN SON"

The feelings and emotions Joseph and Mary experienced at that moment of the Savior's birth can only be visualized by reading between the lines of the few words recorded in Luke: "She brought forth her firstborn son" (JST, Luke 2:8). Elder Jeffrey Holland captured so beautifully the human drama of what they might have been feeling in Bethlehem:

> As a father I have recently begun to think more often of Joseph, that strong, silent, almost unknown man who must have been more worthy than any other mortal man to be the guiding foster father to the living Son of God. It was Joseph selected from among all men who would teach Jesus to work. It was Joseph who taught him the books of the law. It was Joseph who, in the seclusion of the shop, helped him begin to understand who he was and ultimately what he was to become.
>
> I was a student at BYU just finishing my first year of graduate work when our first child, a son, was born. We were very poor, though not so poor as Joseph and Mary. My wife and I were both going to school, both holding jobs, and in addition worked as head residents in an off-campus apartment complex to help defray our rent. We drove a little Volkswagen which had a half-dead battery because we couldn't afford a new one (Volkswagen or battery).
>
> Nevertheless, when I realized that our own night of nights was coming, I believe I would have done any honorable thing in this world, and mortgaged any future I had, to make sure my wife had the clean sheets, the sterile utensils, the attentive nurses, and the skilled doctors who brought forth our firstborn son. If she or that child had needed special care at the Mayo Clinic, I believe I would have ransomed my very life to get it.
>
> I compare those feelings (which I have had with each succeeding child) with what Joseph must have felt as he moved through the streets of a city not his own, with not a friend or kinsman in sight, nor anyone willing to extend a helping hand. In these very last and most painful hours of her "confinement," Mary had ridden or walked

approximately 100 miles from Nazareth in Galilee to Bethlehem in Judea. Surely Joseph must have wept at her silent courage. Now, alone and unnoticed, they had to descend from human company to a stable, a grotto full of animals, there to bring forth the Son of God.[5]

SWADDLING CLOTHES

From Luke, the Greek-minded physician, we learn that Mary wrapped her firstborn son in swaddling clothes. Thus the baby Jesus followed the custom of poor people of His own Palestine. Infant children were washed and rubbed with salt to prevent infection. The baby would then be placed diagonally on a square piece of cloth. Two corners were turned across its sides and feet; then, with the baby's legs together and its arms at its side, it was wound around tightly with linen or cotton bands of cloth, four to five inches wide and five to six yards long. During the day the swaddling bands were loosened and the child was rubbed with olive oil and dusted with powdered myrtle leaves. Swaddling continued until the child was several months old. "The little Palestinian 'papoose' of Christ's time— and today—was more conveniently carried to work on his mother's back in a woolen cradle than if his feet were free. At night his wool cradle swung from two forked sticks."[6] The Prophet Ezekiel indicated that these same customs were practiced in his day at a child's birth: "In the day thou wast born . . . thou wast not washed in water to cleanse thee; thou wast not salted at all, nor swaddled at all" (Ezekiel 16:4, American Revised Version). Christian mothers in Bethlehem still swaddle their babies with neat, narrow bands of colorful material with the band drawn under the baby's chin to teach it to breathe through its nose.

"AND LAID HIM IN A MANGER"

The Greek word for *manger* is *grotto* or *cavern*—a simple cave carved back into the limestone hillside with a wicker gate placed across the front of it where the animals were kept. The Lamb of God (John 1:29) was literally born in a stable and laid in a manger (Luke 2:7, 12).

Bridging the gap between our modern view of a "manger" and the Middle Eastern setting surrounding the Savior's birth, Gerald N. Lund helps increase our understanding of what really took place:

> Two common, but mistaken, ideas have arisen from this verse. First, in modern nativity scenes, the manger is usually in a wooden stable. This imagery comes from European farm life. The traditional site of the Nativity in Bethlehem, however, is a grotto, an underground

limestone cavern. Such grottos were commonly used for housing animals at that time.

Second, the word *inn* brings to mind the quaint, rustic inns of medieval Europe. Typical inns in the Middle East, however, were khans, or caravansaries—small fortresses with high walls and a large open courtyard where the animals spent the night. The "rooms" in such khans were not enclosures at all but a series of arched alcoves in a wall. The members of each group were able to watch their animals and baggage from their "rooms." In busy times, such as at Passover or the census (and both were going on at the time of Jesus' birth), a caravansary would be a chaotic madhouse, and very likely more than one group would be sharing an alcove because of the number of people. There would be no privacy for giving birth to a baby under such conditions, and that may have been the reason Joseph and Mary willingly accepted the more private stable. The picture of the hard-hearted innkeeper callously turning away a woman nine months pregnant is not justified by the scriptural record.[7]

The Savior taught us to humble ourselves, that whosoever would, should be exalted (Matthew 23:12), and He came into the word in the humblest of all circumstances (Luke 2:7).[8]

NO ROOM FOR HIM

Isn't it interesting that Christ created this world, this magnificent planet for all of us, yet when He came to earth, there was no room for Him . . . anywhere. The Joseph Smith Translation of the Bible changes the word *inn* to read there was no room for him in the *inns* (see JST, Luke 2:7).

"Do we get a pang of conscience," Elder Thomas S. Monson asked, "as we recall his own words, ' . . . foxes have holes, and the birds of the air have nests; but the Son of man hath not where to lay his head'? (Matthew 8:20). Or do we flush with embarrassment when we remember, 'And she brought forth her firstborn son . . . and laid him in a manger; because there was no room for them in the inn' (Luke 2:7). No room. No room. No room. Ever has it been."[9]

He placed this earth in a perfect orbit to sustain our lives to become the home for our mortal probation (1 Nephi 17:34)—yet when He was born, there was no room for Him! "Jesus, the God of the whole earth, the very God who created 'the heavens and the earth and all that in them are' was born in a cave. The executor of the Father's word who created worlds without number and brought myriads of planets whirling into existence—born in a cave. The Mighty Jehovah, by whom the suns and planets course through the heavens and are sustained in orbit by His power, the divine source and redeemer of all life teeming on worlds innumerable to man—born in a cave."[10] His humble birth itself bears witness of His meekness. Surrounded that night by all the works of His hands, with only the stars looking down on Him in a crude manger, "He was," Elder Maxwell observed, "in a sense, cradled in His own creations."[11]

Only a few wise men and shepherds were all that paid attention to His birth. As we rush about with the multitude of shoppers and the large Christmas crowds, we can sense what Bethlehem must have been like. Just as there was no room in the inn for Mary, great with child, many today find it hard to make room for Christ in their daily lives and once-a-year celebrations. But our Eternal Life hinges on our willingness to believe in Him and keep His commandments. Nothing else has the power to perfect a life but His divine presence. "Though Christ a thousand times in Bethlehem be born, if He is not born in thee, thy soul is still forlorn." But, happily, if we study His teachings and live His commandments we will also need to make room for the blessings that will come to fill our lives with joy!

Part of leaving Him room at Christmas is to just enjoy and treasure every busy moment, to save them as sweet memories and ammunition for the days that lie ahead.

Notes

1. See the LDS Topical Guide, s.v. "Jesus Christ, Firstborn," 247.
2. See *The Growing Edge*, Church Educational System newsletter, vol. 14 (Dec. 1981).
3. Ibid.
4. Bruce R. McConkie, "A God Is Born," Christmas devotional in the Salt Lake Tabernacle, Dec. 11, 1980, typescript, Church Historical Department, Salt Lake City, Utah, 4, 15.
5. Jeffrey R. Holland, "Maybe Christmas Doesn't Come From A Store," *Ensign*, Dec. 1977, 64–65.
6. Madeleine S. and J. Lane Miller, *Encyclopedia of Bible Life*, (New York: Harper and Brothers Publishers, 1944), 60.
7. *The Growing Edge.*
8. Ibid.
9. Thomas S. Monson, in *Conference Report*, Oct. 1965, 143.

10. I am indebted to Brother Stephen K. Iba, Area Director in Church Education, for this insight. He shared it in a Christmas card to Church Educators in Salt Lake City, Dec. 19, 1988.
11. Elder Neal A. Maxwell, from an unpublished fireside address to LDSSA students in Symphony Hall, Salt Lake City, Utah, Dec. 1991.

THIRTEEN

While Shepherds Watched

*And there were in the same country, shepherds abiding in the field,
keeping watch over their flocks by night.* (JST, Luke 2:8)

JESUS IS THE GOOD SHEPHERD (see John 10:11, 14). He so
designated himself when as Jehovah he inspired King David to write,
"The Lord is my Shepherd" (Psalm 23:1).[1] The Lamb of God was
born during the Passover season when male lambs, without spot or blemish, were sacrificed to God, so it was fitting that shepherds were the first
to receive the announcement of His birth.

Isaiah prophesied that when the Messiah would come, He would
"feed his flock like a shepherd" (Isaiah 40:11). This is so profoundly symbolic: True shepherds come to the Lamb of God, and He, as the Good
Shepherd, has commanded them to "Feed my lambs" (John 21:15).

But these were no ordinary shepherds. When the angels appeared
to announce Christ's birth, the shepherds referred to in the scriptures
may have been keeping watch over the Passover lambs, the very flocks
destined for sacrifice as a type of Christ. As one commentator observed,
"There was near Bethlehem, on the road to Jerusalem, a tower known
as Migdal Eder, or the watch-tower of the flock. Here was the station
where shepherds watched the flock destined for sacrifice in the temple.
. . . It was a settled conviction among the Jews that the Messiah was
to be born in Bethlehem, and equally that he was to be revealed from

Migdal Eder. The beautiful significance of the revelation of the infant Christ to shepherds watching the flocks destined for sacrifice needs no comment."[2]

TIDINGS OF JOY

> And lo, an angel of the Lord appeared unto them, and the glory of the Lord shone round about them; and they were sore afraid.
>
> But the angel said unto them, Fear not, for behold, I bring you good tidings of great joy, which shall be to all people.
>
> For unto you is born this day, in the city of David, a Savior, who is Christ the Lord. (JST, Luke 2:9–11)

The Savior's mission and message was to bring "good tidings of great joy" to all people. It is more than coincidence that, in Greek, the word *gospel* literally means "good news" and, as President David O. McKay noted, "such is the news that emanates from above."[3] The good news is that Christ has come to earth and made an atonement for all mankind—literally an "at-one-ment"—making it possible for all those who desire to return to the presence of our Heavenly Father. The shepherds were among the few in the world's history who were so in tune with the heavens that they could receive that good news directly from God. And "although we cannot say what language the angel used to address the shepherds that night, it was most likely Aramaic (a form of Hebrew), since that was the shepherd's common tongue. In Hebrew, *Savior* is *Yeshua*, another play on the name Jesus. The word *Christ* comes from the Greek *christos*, meaning *anointed one*. The Hebrew equivalent is *meshiach*, which in English is *Messiah*. Because of the sacredness of Jehovah's name, the ancient Hebrews used a substitute title *Adonai*, which is translated *Lord*. The word clearly referred to Jehovah. It is therefore very likely that the angel said that in the city of David was born *Yeshua*, the *Meschiach*, who was *Adonai*. Little wonder the shepherds were electrified."[4]

LYING IN A MANGER

Luke continues his account of the angel's announcement to the shepherds:

> And this is the way you shall find the babe, he is wrapped in swaddling clothes, and is lying in a manger. And suddenly there was with the angel, a multitude of the heavenly host, praising God. (JST, Luke 2:12–13).

The birth of any child is an exciting and wonderful event, but the birth of this baby was spectacular. In the premortal existence the Father presented the plan for our exaltation—not just *a* plan, but *"the great plan"* (Alma 34:9; emphasis added) of mercy and redemption—which would satisfy the demands of the law of justice at the day of judgment, and encircle us in the arms of the Savior's love, mercy, and Atonement (see Alma 34:15–16, 31). It is interesting to note that the word *plan* does not appear in the Bible, neither the Old nor the New Testament, one single time. Yet in the scriptures of the Restoration, the word *plan* appears numerous times.[5]

The Father announced that His plan for our salvation would require a propitiation (or substitute) be made or else all mankind must unavoidably perish (because none of us would be able to pay for all our sins ourself) (Alma 34:9). He declared that someone would have to make an "infinite and eternal" sacrifice, and that they would have to do it willingly. We were overwhelmed with Christ's love for us as we heard Him say, "Here I am, send me" (Abraham 3:27) and "Father, thy will be done, and the glory be thine forever" (Moses 4:2). Elder Maxwell reverently reminded us of how great the Savior's wisdom and His love was at that moment: "Never has anyone offered so much to so many in so few words as when Jesus said 'Here am I, send me.' "[6]

Oh, how we loved Him. His birth would lead to the one event that could keep our heavenly family together throughout all eternity—the Atonement. If we sang together and shouted for joy after hearing of this marvelous plan of salvation and the completion of this earth (see Job 38:4–7), would there not have also arisen a mighty shout of joy and singing when the Son left for earth to put into motion the events that would bring about that plan? "Is it unreasonable to suppose that modern Latter-day Saints were part of the heavenly multitude who sang to righteous shepherds on the hills of Bethlehem that night?"[7]

> *And there was with the angel a multitude of the heavenly host praising God, and saying, Glory to God in the highest; and on earth, peace; goodwill to men.* (JST, Luke 2:14)

When you hear Christmas music being sung, it's not hard to imagine what those heavenly hosts must have sounded like. The melodies and messages of "It Came Upon a Midnight Clear," "Hark the Herald Angels Sing," and "Far Far Away on Judea's Plains" touch us deeply.

Beautiful music is love in search of a soul. "May the glad refrain of the angelic host at the Savior's birth become a universal chorus," the First Presidency (Joseph F. Smith, Anthon H. Lund, and Charles W. Penrose) wrote in 1911, "reverberating over the whole earth, and be materialized in the lives of mankind, paving the way to the coming of the great King to reign forever more!"[8]

There will yet be great carols written. The best hymns have not yet been composed. The words, for example, to one of the new songs we will sing at the Second Coming are in the Doctrine and Covenants (see D&C 84:98–102). We have the words, but where the artists and musicians who will compose the most sacred and soul-stirring music ever to be written, fit for such an occasion? Hopefully they are now "in a preparation" (Alma 32:6) and are paying the price so their talents can be called upon sometime in the future.

PEACE ON EARTH

The Greek rendering of the phrase "and on earth, peace, good will toward men" is recorded *peace among men of good will*. Martin Luther's translation of the Bible (which the Prophet Joseph Smith found "to be the most correct translation, and to correspond nearest to the revelations which God" had given to him[9]) renders this verse as "Glory to God in the highest, and on earth *peace among men with whom He is well pleased.*"

We know from the scriptures that peace on earth won't be a reality until Christ's millennial reign. In fact, in this day of nuclear giants and ethical infants, one of the signs of the times preceding the Second Coming is wars and rumors of war. But, peace can be a reality for the righteous, as President J. Reuben Clark, Jr., explained:

> Heralded centuries before his birth as the "Prince of Peace," heavenly angels announced his coming. Modern man sometimes vainly thinks that Jesus' mission was to wipe out war; and scoffers have cried that since war still curses the earth, Christ's mission has failed and Christianity is a blight.
>
> Yet Christ himself sent forth his Twelve, saying: "Think not that I am come to send peace on earth: I came not to send peace, but a sword."
>
> Christ did proclaim a peace—the peace of everlasting righteousness, which is the eternal and mortal enemy of sin. Between righteousness and sin, in whatever form, there can only be unceasing war, whether in one man, among the people, or between nations in armed

conflict. This war is the sword of Christ; whatever its form this war cannot end until sin is crushed and Christ brings all flesh under his dominion. Righteousness is peace wherever it abides; sin in itself is war wherever it is found.[10]

At Christmastime, the hearts of many yearn for peace on earth. Ironically, though, peace seems so fragile and illusive, even during the holiday when we honor the Prince of Peace. Peace is possible, but not in the world's way. "Peace I leave with you, my peace I give unto you: not as the world giveth, give I unto you. Let not your heart be troubled, neither let it be afraid" (John 14:27). His way is not popular with selfish leaders of nations and groups. His way to peace comes by humble submission to commandments, by giving "glory to God," and by yielding our will to His.

Everything we can do to assist the Father and His Son in their "work and glory, to bring to pass the immortality and eternal life of man" (Moses 1:39), by helping to promote the peace that comes from obedience to the gospel, is worth our best effort. It is always a privilege to do anything for the Lord. And there is no greater work to be done anywhere in the world than His. President John Taylor testified, "Our feelings towards the world of mankind, generally, ought to be the same as Jesus manifested to them. He sought to promote their welfare, and our motto ought ever to be the same as his was—'Peace on earth and good will to men'; no matter who they are or what they are, we should seek to promote the happiness and welfare of all Adam's race."[11] John Taylor said, "We have never entertained any other feeling or principle than this; nor do we desire to cherish any unhallowed feelings in our bosoms either to individuals or the nation."[12]

We simply cannot do His work our way. To illustrate, in 1842 the Prophet Joseph Smith wrote about mankind's frail attempts and failures to obtain peace versus the Lord's way:

> The government of God has always tended to promote peace, unity, harmony, strength, and happiness: while that of man has been productive of confusion, disorder, weakness, and misery. The greatest acts of the mighty men have been to depopulate nations and to overthrow kingdoms: and whilst they have exalted themselves and become glorious, it has been at the expense of the lives of the innocent, the blood of the oppressed, the moans of the widow, and the tears of the orphan. . . .
>
> The designs of God, on the other hand, have been to promote the universal good of the universal world; to establish peace and good will among men, to promote the principles of eternal truth; to bring about

a state of things that shall unite man to his fellow man; cause the world to "beat their swords into plowshares, and their spears into pruning hooks' [and to] make the nations of the earth dwell in peace. . . ."[13]

Attempts to promote universal peace and happiness in the human family have proved abortive; every effort has failed; every plan and design has fallen to the ground; it needs the wisdom of God, the intelligence of God, and the power of God to accomplish this.[14]

Ironically, it is during times of great stress and social unrest when people pen priceless poems about peace. Joseph Smith received the great revelation and prophecy on war—foretelling the day when "war shall be poured out upon all nations"—on Christmas day! (See D&C 87.) Similarly, during the Civil War, the poet Longfellow was so upset about the lack of peace on earth that he penned his immortal "Christmas Bells." He had just learned that his son, a young lieutenant, had been wounded in a battle at Gettysburg, Virginia. On Christmas day, as the church bells began to ring, Longfellow began to write. Five of the seven original stanzas of his poem are in our modern hymn "I Heard the Bells," but they are in an inverted order.

Lyrics	Verse Number in LDS Hymn Book
I heard the bells on Christmas Day Their old, familiar carols play, And wild and sweet The words repeat Of peace on earth, good-will to men!	1
And thought how, as the day had come, The belfries of all Christendom Had rolled along The unbroken song Of peace on earth, good-will to men!	2
Till, ringing, singing on its way, The world revolved from night to day, A voice, a chime, A chant sublime Of peace on earth, good-will to men!	5

Then from each black, accursed mouth
The cannon thundered in the South,
And with the sound
The carols drowned
Of peace on earth, good-will to men!

It was as if an earthquake rent
The hearth-stones of a continent,
And made forlorn
The households born
Of peace on earth, good-will to men!

And in despair I bowed my head;   3
"There is no peace on earth," I said;
"For hate is strong,
And mocks the song
Of peace on earth, good-will to men!"

Then pealed the bells more loud and deep: 4
"God is not dead; nor doth he sleep!
The Wrong shall fail,
The Right prevail,
With peace on earth, good-will to men!"

This hymn, as it stands in our hymn book, is inspiring. But when read as originally penned, it becomes more than just a Christmas carol. It becomes another testament that Christ can end war and establish peace. Prophets have always known that the permanent solution to war has to be centered in Christ. Isaiah, for example, saw wars coming to his own people (the tribe of Judah), to the northern ten tribes of Israel, and to our day. The same solution that all the prophets have seen was shown to him: obedience to the commandments of the Messiah. That's why, in the middle of his prophecies of doom on a nation, Isaiah burst into song: "Behold a virgin shall conceive, and bear a son, and shall call his name Immanuel. . . . For unto us a child is born, unto us a son is given: and the government shall be upon his shoulder and his name shall be called

Wonderful, Counsellor, The Mighty God, The Everlasting Father, The Prince of Peace" (Isaiah 7:14 and 9:6).

The key to solving the contentions raging in the world today is the same as it was then—obey Christ, live His gospel. There is no other way. It worked for the Nephite/Lamanite conflicts (see Alma 24), it exterminated gangs and secret combinations (see Helaman 6:37), and it will eventually solve the Arab/Israeli crisis (see 2 Nephi 6:11; 9:2; 10:7; and 3 Nephi 20:29–37). No country can be established in their homeland in peace until they fully accept Christ and His gospel. When they do obey, Isaiah declared, peace will come. For "the work of the righteousness shall be peace; and the effect of righteousness quietness and assurance for ever. And my people shall dwell in a peaceable habitation, and in sure dwellings, and in quiet resting places" (Isaiah 32:17–18).

We fully expect our government leaders to have virtues, but societal safety can only be guaranteed when "virtue resides in the people as well as in the leaders."[15] Speaking symbolically—we have a Statue of Liberty on the East Coast; perhaps we should erect a Statue of Responsibility on the West Coast, as a reminder that liberty will not last long without responsible behavior. The keys for obtaining His peace and safety have been revealed through His prophets: "Learn of me, and listen to my words; walk in the meekness of my Spirit, and you shall have peace in me. I am Jesus Christ; I came by the will of the Father, and I do His will" (D&C 19:23–24). As President McKay said, " 'Peace on earth, good will toward men' may become a reality by compliance to the principles of the gospel."[16] "It is the spirit of the gospel of Jesus Christ, obedience to which will bring 'peace on earth,' because it means . . . good will toward men."[17] On another occasion, President McKay prayed, "May each Christmas find the members of the Church truer, purer, and nobler than the last, that they with minds and hearts united may hasten the day when the Lord will bless his people with peace."[18]

Peace can be ours, as individuals, as families, and as nations, only if we live the gospel. The earth will experience its greatest day of peace during the great Millennium, when "men shall beat their swords into plowshares, and their spears into pruninghooks [and] nation shall not lift up sword against nation, neither shall they learn war any more" (Isaiah 2:4). The faster the gospel of Jesus Christ can move around the world, the greater the peace will be. "Wherefore, labor ye, labor ye in my vineyard for the last time—for the last time call upon the inhabitants of the earth.

For in mine own due time will I come upon the earth in judgment, and my people shall be redeemed and shall reign with me on earth. For the great Millennium [of peace], of which I have spoken by the mouth of my servants, shall come" (D&C 43:28–30).

"LET US GO AND SEE"

Luke adds an important spiritual note about what the shepherds did with the information they had received from the angels:

> *And it came to pass, when the angels were gone away from them into heaven, the shepherds said one to another, Let us now go, even unto Bethlehem, and see this thing which is come to pass, which the Lord has made known unto us. And they came with haste.* (JST, Luke 2:15).

Why do you imagine the shepherds went *with haste* to see the newborn child? Do we respond so readily to the promptings of the Spirit? Why would the Lord bless those who do not hesitate to do what is right? Like these good shepherds, we too can go to Bethlehem, in our minds and hearts, and see the Christ child. Two of the best roads leading to Bethlehem, spiritually, are reading the scriptures and serving others as He would have done.

> *And [the shepherds] found Mary and Joseph, and the babe lying in a manger.*
> *And when they had seen, they made known abroad the saying which was told them concerning this child.* (JST, Luke 2:16–17)

They told everybody! They shared their witness with all who would listen. And why not? This was the most momentous event to occur since the Fall of Adam. The gift of testimony they shared is one that all of us can share with our families and friends at Christmas. Like these good shepherds, we, too, can "stand as witnesses of God at all times and in all things, and in all places that ye may be in" (Mosiah 18:9).

> *All they who heard it, wondered at those things which were told them by the shepherds.* (JST, Luke 2:18)

These shepherds must have also wondered at the things that were told them by the angels. But they did more than wonder—they acted. They went to see for themselves who this Savior was, just as each of us must do. May we, who stand as His under-shepherds in our respective "fields" of labor in His kingdom, who have seen His star, humbly lead others to His side, to behold Him.[19]

And the shepherds returned, glorifying and praising God for all the things which they had heard and seen, as they were manifested unto them." (JST Luke 2:20)

The shepherds teach us that we can take a glorious gift away from Christmas to keep throughout the year—a sense of God's power, goodness, and mercy, and a dedication to His work. We can, like the shepherds of Bethlehem, return to our own fields of labor filled with the kind of love that leads to godly actions.

MARY KEPT ALL THESE THINGS IN HER HEART

But Mary kept all these things and pondered them in her heart. (JST Luke 2:19)

If Mary kept all these things in her heart, how, then, did they come to be written in the Gospel of Luke? This is especially interesting when we consider that Luke's gospel may have been written many years after the crucifixion of Jesus Christ.

We don't know for certain, but several Christian commentaries suggest that Luke may have actually met Mary and interviewed her. After the Savior's ascension, the Church He established began to experience severe persecution. Peter was crucified (upside down, according to tradition).[20] James was beheaded (in about AD 44).[21] John the Beloved (also called John the Revelator) was the only member of the First Presidency who survived, and is believed to have become president of the Church after Peter's death.

Church headquarters were moved from Jerusalem to Ephesus,[22] and tradition has it that Mary, the mother of Jesus, moved there in her later years.[23] That would be probable because Jesus, while suffering on the cross, had given John the responsibility to care for his mother with the words, "Son, behold thy mother" (John 19:27). John was later promised by the Savior that he would never taste of death (see D&C 7), thus making him the most appropriate choice to care for His mother.

Later, Luke was Paul's missionary companion (see Luke 20), and at Miletus they sent for the elders of Ephesus to come and meet with them. Luke probably had the opportunity, Christian historians have suggested, to meet Mary while serving with Paul, either in Jerusalem later or in Ephesus. His account of the birth of Christ is so much more detailed than the other Gospels. Perhaps that is why Luke chapter 2 is universally accepted as *the* Christmas story, because it may possibly be Mary's story, much more personal and detailed concerning that sacred event.

Notes

1. The translators of the King James Version used the word LORD, in all capital letters to render the Hebrew holy tetragram "JHV" for *Yahweh* or *Jehovah*; and thus a proper reading might be, "Jehovah is my shepherd." See Gerald N. Lund, *Jesus Christ, Key to the Plan of Salvation* (Salt Lake City: Deseret Book, 1991), 18.

2. See Marvin R. Vincent, *Word Studies in the New Testament* (Eerdman's Publishing, 1980), 1:142; as quoted in *The Growing Edge*, Church Educational System newsletter, vol. 14 (Dec. 1981).

3. David O. McKay, in *Conference Report*, Apr. 1910, 106.

4. *The Growing Edge.*

5. The word *plan* does not appear in either the Old or New Testaments. But it does appear numerous times in the Book of Mormon and once in the Pearl of Great Price: The plan of redemption (Alma 12:26, 12:30, 12:32, 12:33, 17:16, 18:39, 29:2, 39:18, 41:2, 42:11, 42:13); The great plan of redemption (Jacob 6:8, Alma 34:31); The great and eternal plan of redemption (Alma 34:16); The plan of redemption which was prepared from the foundation of the world (Alma 12:25, 22:13); The plan of salvation (Jarom 1:2, Alma 24:14, Moses 6:62); The great plan of salvation (Alma 42:5); The plan of happiness (Alma 42:16); The great plan of happiness (Alma 42:8); The plan of Mercy (Alma 42:15); The great plan of mercy (Alma 42:31); The plan of restoration (Alma 41:2); The great and eternal plan of deliverance (2 Nephi 11:5); God's eternal plan (D&C Official Declaration 2:9); The great plan of the eternal God (Alma 29:2, 34:9); The merciful plan of the Great Creator (2 Nephi 9:6); O how great the plan of our God (2 Nephi 9:13); And the Gods saw . . . that their plan was good (Abraham 4:21).

6. Neal A. Maxwell, in Conference Report, Apr. 1976, 39.

7. *The Growing Edge.*

8. Christmas Message of the First Presidency (Joseph F. Smith, Anthon H. Lund, Charles W. Penrose), as cited in James R. Clark, *Messages of the First Presidency of The Church of Jesus Christ of Latter-day Saints*, 6 vols. (Salt Lake City: Bookcraft, 1965–75), 4:258.

9. Joseph Smith, *Teachings of the Prophet Joseph Smith*, 349 and 361.

10. J. Reuben Clark Jr., in *Conference Report*, Apr. 1939, 104–105.

11. John Taylor, *Journal of Discourses*, 14:188.

12. John Taylor, *Journal of Discourses*, 22:139.

13. Joseph Smith, *Teachings of the Prophet Joseph Smith*, 248, 252.

14. See Joseph Smith, *Teachings of the Prophet Joseph Smith*, 252.

15. Elder Neal A. Maxwell, quoted in "America, God Mend Thine Every Flaw," *LDS Church News,* 10 July 1993, 4.

16. David O. McKay, in *Conference Report*, April 1963, 98.

17. David O. McKay, *Gospel Ideals* (Salt Lake City: Deseret Book, 1953), 551.

18. David O. McKay, "Of Peace—and Christ—and Christmas," *Improvement Era,* 57, Dec. 1954, 862.

19. The thought expressed in this sentence comes from Steven K. Iba's Christmas card to Church Educators in Salt Lake City, Dec. 1988.

20. See James E. Talmage, *Jesus the Christ,* 219.

21. See *The Life and Teachings of Jesus and His Apostles,* 2nd ed. (Salt Lake City: The Church of Jesus Christ of Latter-day Saints, 1979), 253. See also LDS Bible Dictionary, s.v. "James."

22. *The Life and Teachings,* 452.

23. See "Introduction to Luke," *The Abingdon Bible Commentary,* (New York: Abingdon, 1929), 1025.

FOURTEEN

"Mine Eyes Have Seen"

THE BLESSING AND PROPHECY OF SIMEON

Soon after Christ's birth, Joseph and Mary probably left the stable for the comfort of a simple house. Their baby's circumcision and blessing were performed according to the law of Moses.

> *And when eight days were accomplished for the circumcising of the child, his name was called Jesus; which was so named of the angel, before he was conceived.* (JST, Luke 2:21)

According to the law, Mary remained ritually impure for forty days until Joseph presented two pigeons to a temple priest who offered them as a burnt offering to the Lord. Joseph and Mary then presented the baby Jesus to Simeon, the priest, for the redemption of their firstborn son, for according to the law, all firstborn things belonged to God. Jesus was redeemed by his parents paying five shekels to the priest. Although all firstborn children had to be redeemed in this same manner, this little baby was the only one who truly fulfilled the symbolism of the ceremony because Jesus was the Firstborn of the Father who would redeem mankind.

> *And when the days of her purification, according to the law of Moses, were accomplished; they brought him to Jerusalem, to present him to the Lord;*
>
> *(As it is written in the law of the Lord, Every male which openeth the womb shall be called holy to the Lord;)*

*And to offer a sacrifice according to that which is written in the law of
the Lord, A pair of turtledoves, or two young pigeons.* (Luke 2:22–24)

Simeon had been promised in a revelation that before his death he
would see the Christ. It was fitting that when the infant Jesus was presented to him, that a witness of the Spirit was given:

*And behold, there was a man at Jerusalem, whose name was Simeon;
and the same man was just and devout, waiting for the consolation of
Israel; and the Holy Ghost was upon him.*

*And it was revealed unto him by the Holy Ghost, that he should not
see death before he had seen the Lord's Christ.*

*And he came by the Spirit into the temple; and when the parents
brought in the child, even Jesus, to do for him after the custom of the law,*

Then took he him up in his arms, and blessed God, and said,

Lord, now lettest thy servant depart in peace, according to thy word;

For mine eyes have seen thy salvation,

Which thou hast prepared before the face of all people;

A light to lighten the Gentiles, and the glory of thy people Israel. (JST,
Luke 2:25–32)

These words of Simeon are descriptive of the Savior and His mission: "a light to lighten the Gentiles, and the glory of thy people Israel."
As members of the house of Israel in these last days, we, too, have been
"prepared" in the premortal life and foreordained to fulfill certain covenants. In a revelation given to the Prophet Joseph in December 1832,
the Lord echoed the words of Simeon in outlining the duties of the Saints
who desire to join with Christ in becoming "saviors on Mount Zion" (see
Obadiah 1:21 and D&C 103:9):

Therefore, thus saith the Lord unto you, with whom the priesthood
hath continued through the lineage of your fathers—For ye are lawful
heirs, according to the flesh, and have been hid from the world with
Christ in God—Therefore your life and the priesthood have remained,
and must needs remain through you and your lineage until the restoration
of all things spoken by the mouths of all the holy prophets since the world
began. Therefore, blessed are ye if ye continue in my goodness, *a light unto
the Gentiles*, and through this priesthood, *a savior unto my people Israel.*
The Lord hath said it. Amen. (D&C 86:8–11; emphasis added)

These few verses outline the entire mission of the Church—to invite
all to come unto Christ by perfecting our lives, sharing the gospel, and

redeeming the dead. Elder Theodore M. Burton gave us some important insights into the meaning of these verses of scripture:

> In this scripture the Lord was not talking about your priesthood line of authority. He was talking about your inherited right to receive and use priesthood power. This readiness to listen and believe is an inherited gift which enabled you to recognize and accept the truth. Jesus explained this thought as he said: "My sheep hear my voice, and I know them, and they follow me." That spirit of acceptance is a manifestation of your inherited right to priesthood blessings. Such willingness to believe does not represent predestination, but it does represent foreordination. The Lord continues the revelation: "For ye are lawful heirs, according to the flesh, and have been hid from the world with Christ in God." This means we receive a right to priesthood blessings from our blood ancestry. I hope you can understand that priesthood with its accompanying blessings is dependent to a great degree on family relationship. In this final verse the Lord reminds us of two things. First, he reminds us of our responsibility to do missionary work here on the earth. Second, he informs us that we are not only to be messengers of salvation to the living, but saviors for our ancestors who went before us and who, though now dead, have paved the way whereby we might receive our present blessings. It is through them we received our priesthood. The promise was made that even if they were born at a time and place where they could not hear the gospel preached in life, God would provide saviors for them from among their descendants. We are those saviors God promised through whom they can have every priesthood blessing.[1]

Elder John A. Widtsoe explained that we made specific promises and covenants in the premortal life to become "saviors" by building temples and providing ordinances:

> In our pre-existent state, in the day of the great council, we made a certain agreement with the Almighty. The Lord proposed a plan, conceived by him. We accepted it. Since the plan is intended for all men, we become parties to the salvation of every person under the plan. We agreed, right then and there, to be not only saviors for ourselves, but measurably saviors for the whole human family. We went into a partnership with the Lord. The working out of the plan became then not merely the Father's work, and Savior's work, but also our work. The least of us, the humblest, is in partnership with the Almighty in achieving the purpose of the eternal plan of salvation by providing them with temple ordinances, which they could not obtain on their own.[2]

Luke's sacred account of Simeon's prophecy continues:

>   *And Joseph, and Mary, marveled at those things which were spoken of the child. And Simeon blessed them, and said unto Mary, Behold, this child is set for the fall and rising again of many in Israel; and for a sign which shall be spoken against; Yea, a spear shall pierce through him to the wounding of thine own soul also; that the thoughts of many hearts may be revealed.* (JST Luke 2:22–35)

Note Simeon's statement that a spear would pierce him and bring anguish to Mary's soul. We can scarcely imagine the anguish of his mother when Jesus, hanging on the cross, looked down at Mary and said, in fulfillment of Simeon's words, "Woman, behold thy son!" (John 19:26).

THE PROPHECY OF ANNA

Anna was "a woman who received revelation from the Holy Ghost certifying that Jesus is the Christ."[3] She was therefore a "prophetess" (see Revelation 19:10).

>   *And there was one Anna, a prophetess, the daughter of Phanuel, of the tribe of Aser. She was of a great age, and had lived with a husband only seven years, whom she married in her youth,*
>   *And she lived a widow of about fourscore and four years, who departed not from the temple, but served God with fastings and prayers, night and day.*
>   *And she, coming in that instant, gave thanks likewise unto the Lord, and spake of him, to all those who looked for redemption in Jerusalem.* (JST, Luke 2:36–38).

If Anna married at an early age (a common occurrence at that time), had lived with a husband for seven years, and then as a widow for another eighty-four years, she could have been almost a hundred years of age at the time she saw the Christ child. She, no doubt, had waited years to behold this blessed Babe. Blessings are never denied the righteous. They are sometimes delayed, but never denied. Her patience and faith was rewarded. She was "a woman who . . . received revelation from the Holy Ghost certifying that Jesus is the Christ."[4]

>   *And when they had performed all things according to the law of the Lord, they returned into Galilee to their own city, Nazareth.* (JST, Luke 2:39).

THE WISE MEN SEEK THE CHRIST CHILD

The Magi from the East followed the new light in the heavens, literally fulfilling a prophecy of Isaiah's given seven hundred years earlier: "For, behold, the darkness shall cover the earth, and gross darkness the people: but the Lord shall arise upon thee, and his glory shall be seen upon thee. And the Gentiles shall come to thy light, and kings to the brightness of thy rising. . . . The multitude of camels shall cover thee, the dromedaries [camels of unusual speed and breeding] of Midian and Ephah; all they from Sheba shall come: they shall bring gold and incense; and they shall shew forth the praises of the Lord" (Isaiah 60:2–3, 6).

Matthew recorded the event as follows:

> *Now when Jesus was born in Bethlehem of Judea, in the days of Herod the king, behold, there came wise men from the east to Jerusalem, Saying, Where is the child that is born, the Messiah of the Jews? for we have seen his star in the east, and have come to worship him.* (JST, Matthew 3:1–2).

Tradition has led us to place wise men and their camels in the manger scene the night Christ was born, but the scriptures teach that they came to Bethlehem some time after His birth. Matthew 3:7 states that Herod asked when the star appeared and ordered the death of all children under age two, so we assume that the wise men may have searched for Jesus as long as two years. Also, when the wise men visited the family, Joseph and Mary were living in a house (no longer in a stable), and Jesus is called a "young child" no less than ten times (see vv. 8–21). If our Christmas creches were doctrinally correct, we would place the wise men in the other room, heading toward the manger!

There has been much speculation about the wise men from the east who visited Joseph, Mary, and the young child Jesus in Bethlehem. Christian midrash (legend) is replete with suggestions as to the wise men, their countries, their names, even their numbers. Were the eastern visitors from Persia, Arabia, or Mesopotamia? The assumption is that they were three in number because of the three gifts they presented. From the brief scriptural account in the Gospel of Matthew, we know very little about these Magi who came "from a land east of Palestine to pay homage to the new-born Messiah. . . . [But] these were certainly not ordinary men," an *LDS Church News* editorial suggested. "They were not mere astrologers as some have assumed. They were more likely righteous men who knew the prophecies of the birth of Christ and who were able to discern the new star that appeared in the heavens. . . . That they were spiritual men is evident by the fact that after their encounter with the wicked King Herod they were warned of God in a dream not to re-visit Herod but to return home by another route. This they did, in response to the spiritual counsel that came to them."[5]

"As to the men themselves, one thing is clear," Elder McConkie wrote. "They had prophetic insight. It was with them as it had been with saintly Simeon. . . . They knew the King of the Jews had been born, and they knew that a new star was destined to arise and had arisen in connection with that birth. The probability is they were themselves Jews who lived, as millions of Jews then did, in one of the nations to the East. It was the Jews, not the Gentiles, who were acquainted with the scriptures and who were waiting with anxious expectation for the coming of a King."[6]

Another striking thought about these wise men is that they were sent as witnesses. They sought counsel from others as to where they might find the Messiah (JST, Matthew 3:2), they came to see for themselves, and then they returned bearing witness, no doubt, of all they had seen. They received fragmented information from wicked King Herod, which, fortunately, was enough to lead them to Bethlehem. In our day, however, we are blessed to have true prophets and apostles who can righteously lead us to Christ without a lot of wandering and searching based on partially correct information. They have been called by prophecy and revelation to bring us to Christ and can help us make Him the center of our lives. That's why President Brigham Young was inspired to have Ursa Major, the Big Bear, commonly known as the Big Dipper, inscribed on the west wall of the Salt Lake Temple. Ursa Major points unfailingly to the North Star, a star firmly fixed in the heavens around which all the other stars in the galaxy turn. Mariners have used it to guide them through vast areas of unchartered wilderness and sea. The living prophet is, figuratively speaking, like the North Star to us. As we look to leadership and counsel of the living prophet of God today, we can be pointed to the way of truth and righteousness. He points unfailingly to the Savior, who will give us life eternal.

Like the wise men, we, too, need to have a personal witness of Christ. Each of us must gain a personal knowledge of the truth and be guided by the light within. Elder Henry D. Taylor expressed it this way: "Every member of the Church is entitled to know that God our Heavenly Father lives; that he is not dead. He is also entitled to know that our elder brother, Jesus Christ, is the Savior and Redeemer of the world, and that he has opened the door for us, that we, through our individual acts, may receive salvation and exaltation and dwell once again in the presence of our Heavenly Father. This assurance and witness must be earnestly sought."[7]

In 1856, President Heber C. Kimball, counselor to President Brigham Young, testified, "The time will come when no man nor woman will be able to endure on borrowed light. Each will have to be guided by the light within himself. If you do not have it, how can you stand?"[8]

The wise men's inquiries about the newborn King caused no small stir among those who had no such spiritual witness.

> When Herod the king had heard of the child, he was troubled, and all Jerusalem with him.
>
> And when he had gathered all the chief priests, and scribes of the people together, he demanded of them, saying, Where is the place that is written of by the prophets, in which Christ should be born? For he greatly feared, yet he believed not the prophets.
>
> And they said unto him, It is written by the prophets, that he should be born in Bethlehem of Judea, for thus have they said,
>
> The word of the Lord came unto us, saying, And thou Bethlehem, which lieth in the land of Judea, in thee shall be born a prince, which art not the least among the princes of Judea; for out of thee shall come the Messiah, who shall save my people Israel. (JST, Matthew 3:3–6)

Christ, who was both Shepherd and King to Israel, received homage from shepherds and kings.[9] The King James Version uses the words "King of the Jews" in place of "Messiah" and "rule" instead of "save" "my people Israel." In the Greek, the word *rule* carries more of a connotation of tending, protecting, or nurturing, as a shepherd protects the flock. The same word is used in 2 Samuel 5:2 and in 1 Chronicles 11:2, verses which referred to the fact that Israel's true King would be like a shepherd to His people.[10] (See also John 10:1–15; Ezekiel 34.)

> Then Herod, when he had called the wise men privily, inquired of them diligently what time the star appeared.
>
> And he sent them to Bethlehem, and said, Go and search diligently for the young child; and when ye have found the child, bring me word again, that I may come and worship him also.
>
> When they had heard the king, they departed; and lo, the star which they saw in the east, went before them, until it came and stood over where the young child was.
>
> When they saw the star, they rejoiced with exceeding great joy. (JST, Matthew 3:7–10)

At the birth of Him called the "bright and morning star" (Revelation 22:16), a new star appeared in the heavens.[11]

There seems to be evidence in these and the following verses that not everyone realized the new star had appeared. There was a real star, but apparently, the only ones who saw it were those who were looking for it.[12] They knew from scripture and prophecy that the Messiah was born. Likewise, we must turn to the scriptures to know of Christ and of the rebirth he offers us: "Behold, whosoever believeth on my words, them will I visit with the manifestation of my Spirit; and they shall be born of me, even of water and of the Spirit" (D&C 5:16).

> *And when they were come into the house, they saw the young child, with Mary his mother, and fell down and worshiped him. And when they had opened their treasures, they presented unto him gifts; gold, and frankincense, and myrrh.* (JST, Matthew 3:11)

Their gifts were tokens of love and respect, given to God's greatest gift—His Only Begotten Son (see John 3:16; D&C 34:1, 3). Frankincense is "the fragrant resinous exudation [a white-amber, fragrant gum resin] of various species of boswellia; it was imported into Judea from Arabia. It was an ingredient in the holy incense for sacrificial purposes (see Exodus 30:34) and was highly valued as a perfume."[13] Myrrh was [a yellowish-brown, bitter tasting gum resin from the Arabian rock rose, see Genesis 37:25 and 43:11] "used in preparation of the holy ointment (see Exodus 30:23); in the purification of women (Esther 2:12); as a perfume (Psalm 45:8); and for embalming (John 19:39). It was obtained from various thorny shrubs of the dry districts of Arabia and eastern Africa."[14]

Each of these gifts were symbolic of that Divine Gift and foretold Christ would become the following: gold—a King; frankincense (an incense offered to God)—a high priest; and myrrh (a burial spice)—a healer and a martyr.

Another interesting thought about these gifts is their practical value. Joseph and Mary would shortly be commanded by an angel in a vision to take the Christ child and flee to Egypt for safety. Surely these gifts, arriving just when they did, were a godsend that enabled the holy family to uproot their lives and make their way down to Egypt for the next few years. Having faith in God means that we should also have faith in His timing. And in this case, the timing of the wise men's gifts was perfect to help meet an unforeseen need. It is just as Nephi testified: "The tender mercies of the Lord are over all those whom he hath chosen, because of their faith, to make them mighty, even unto the power of deliverance" (1 Nephi 1:21).

What opportunity do we have to bring Him gifts, to worship Him? The gifts of the wise men teach us that we, too, can bring Christ our gifts out of love and respect. "We can give symbolically our gold, frankincense, and myrrh, first by faithfully paying our tithes and offerings to sustain the Church that bears His name. In the meridian of time, frankincense and myrrh represented sacrifice and purification. We can bring to the Savior our sacrifice and willing service in His Kingdom, and a desire to strive each day to purify our lives and sanctify ourselves before Him so that we may ultimately stand before Him and be comfortable in His presence."[15]

The wise men worshipped the child they sought and then left. God warned them not to return to Herod with the information he desired of them. If they weren't aware of Herod's treachery before, there was no doubt in their minds of it now.

> *And being warned of God in a dream that they should not return to Herod, [the wise men] departed into their own country another way.* (JST, Matthew 3:12).

These truly were wise, intelligent men. The Lord defines intelligence as "light and truth" and declares that "light and truth forsake that evil one." (D&C 93:36–37). To heed the promptings of the Spirit and forsake evil is an act of high intelligence. Our willingness to obey the Lord's commandments is not only an intelligent decision, but also a gift of love to the Savior who declared, "If ye love me, keep my commandments" (John 14:15).

Notes

1. Theodore M. Burton, in *Conference Report*, Apr. 1975, 103, 105.
2. John A. Widtsoe, "The Worth of Souls," *Utah Genealogical and Historical Magazine*, Oct. 1934, 189.
3. Bruce R. McConkie, *Doctrinal New Testament Commentary*, 3 vols. (Salt Lake City: Deseret Book), 1:101.
4. Ibid.
5. "Lessons from the Wise Men," *LDS Church News* editorial, Dec. 16, 1989, p. 16.
6. Bruce R. McConkie, *The Mortal Messiah*, 4 vols. (Salt Lake City: Deseret Book, 1979], 1:358.
7. Henry D. Taylor, in *Conference Report*, Apr. 1971, 158–59.

8. Orson F. Whitney, *Life of Heber C. Kimball*, (1888; reprint, Collector's Edition, Salt Lake City: Bookcraft, 1992), 450.

9. See John 10:11; Revelation 19:16; Matthew 2:11; and Luke 2:15–16; from *The Growing Edge*, Church Educational System newsletter, vol. 14 (Dec. 1981).

10. See *The Growing Edge*.

11. Ibid.

12. Bruce R. McConkie, *The Mortal Messiah*, 1:359.

13. LDS Bible Dictionary, s.v. "Frankincense."

14. LDS Bible Dictionary, s.v. "Myrrh."

15. "Lessons from the Wise Men," *LDS Church News* editorial, Dec. 16, 1989, 16.

FIFTEEN

JESUS' YOUTH

A Time of Preparation

FLIGHT INTO EGYPT

> *And when [the wise men] were departed, behold, the angel of the*
> *Lord, appeared to Joseph in a vision, saying, Arise and take the young child*
> *and his mother, and flee into Egypt, and tarry thou there until I bring thee*
> *word; for Herod will seek the young child to destroy him.*
>
> *And then he arose, and took the young child, and the child's mother,*
> *by night, and departed into Egypt;*
>
> *And was there until the death of Herod, that it might be fulfilled*
> *which was spoken of the Lord, by the prophet, saying, Out of Egypt have I*
> *called my Son.* (JST, Matthew 3:13–15)

This incident had been prophesied by Hosea: "When Israel was a child, then I loved him, and called my son out of Egypt" (Hosea 11:1). The trip to Egypt by the holy family had also been foreshadowed by an event in Israel's history. Nephi wrote that "all things which have been given of God from the beginning of the world, unto men, are the typifying of [Christ]" (2 Nephi 11:4); even specific historical events were designed to foreshadow the coming of Christ. The Old Testament patriarch Joseph was going to be killed by his brothers, but his life was preserved and he was sold into slavery and taken into Egypt. His going to Egypt became the means of salvation for his family. Some eighteen hundred years later, Joseph the Carpenter was commanded to take the Christ child and go to Egypt. Their going to Egypt became the means whereby the Savior's life was preserved, enabling him to carry out his mission to save the entire human family.

SLAUGHTER OF THE CHILDREN IN BETHLEHEM

> *Then Herod, when he saw that he was mocked of the wise men, was exceeding wroth; and sent forth and slew all the children that were in Bethlehem, and all the coasts thereof, from two years old and under, according to the time which he had diligently inquired of the wise men.*
>
> *Then was fulfilled that which was spoken by Jeremiah the prophet, saying,*
>
> *In Ramah there was a voice heard, lamentation, and weeping, and great mourning; Rachael weeping for the loss of her children, and would not be comforted because they were not.* (JST, Matthew 3:16–18)

Given the high infant mortality rate of the day in question and considering the population of Bethlehem to be about one thousand, scholars estimate that the number of male children murdered on this occasion probably did not exceed twenty. "But," writes Alfred Edersheim, "the deed was none the less atrocious; and these infants may justly be regarded as the 'protomartyrs,' the first witnesses of Christ." Continuing, Edersheim remarked: "The slaughter was entirely in accordance with the character and former measures of Herod. Nor do we wonder, that it remained unrecorded by Josephus, since on other occasions also he has omitted events which to us seem important. The murder of a few infants in an insignificant village might appear scarcely worth notice in a reign stained by so much bloodshed."[1]

At this same time, John the Baptist was a small child, just six months older than Jesus. There was good reason for John's being raised in the wilderness of the deserts. The Prophet Joseph Smith taught, "When Herod's edict went forth to destroy the young children, John came under this hellish edict, and Zacharias caused his mother to take him into the mountains, where he was raised on locusts and wild honey. When his father refused to disclose his hiding place, and being the officiating high priest at the Temple that year, was slain by Herod's order, between the porch and the altar, as Jesus said [see Matthew 23:24–25]."[2]

Zacharias unselfishly died to save his son's life. He, along with the children slain in Bethlehem, were the first martyrs of the Christian era.

FROM EGYPT TO NAZARETH

After a few years, when Herod had finally died, the Lord called the holy family out of Egypt and commanded them to go to Nazareth. This move helped to fulfill three important prophecies about Jesus: (1) He would be born in Bethlehem; (2) He would come from Egypt; and (3) He would be called a Nazarene.

> But when Herod was dead, behold, an angel of the Lord appeared in a vision to Joseph in Egypt,
> Saying, Arise, and take the young child and his mother, and go into the land of Israel; for they are dead who sought the young child's life.
> And he arose, and took the young child and his mother, and came into the land of Israel.
> But when he heard that Archelaus did reign in Judea, in the stead of his father Herod, he was afraid to go thither; but, notwithstanding, being warned of God in a vision, he went into the eastern part of Galilee;
> And he came and dwelt in a city called Nazareth, that it might be fulfilled which was spoken by the prophets, He shall be called a Nazarene.
> (JST, Matthew 3:19–23)

FROM GRACE TO GRACE

It was here in the mountainous village of Nazareth that Jesus spent his childhood and learned to follow in His fathers' (plural) footsteps—He became a carpenter with Joseph, and He prepared himself to follow His Heavenly Father.

> And it came to pass that Jesus grew up with his brethren, and waxed strong, and waited upon the Lord for the time of his ministry to come.
> And he served under his father. (JST, Matthew 3:24–25)

> And the child grew, and waxed strong in spirit, being filled with wisdom, and the grace of God was upon him. (JST, Luke 2:40)

Even though He was eventually visited and taught by heavenly beings, Jesus, like all who are born into mortality, had a normal childhood. He was cloaked with the veil of forgetfulness common to all who are born to earth. He gradually learned who He was and what He was to do. John the Baptist said, "He received not of the fulness at the first, but received grace for grace; And he . . . continued from grace to grace, until he received a fulness; And thus he was called the Son of God, because he received not of the fulness at the first." (See D&C 93:12–14.) His growth was not from "sin" to "grace" as is ours, but "from grace to grace"!

"Grace" refers to the gifts and powers of God by which men can be brought to perfection. To say that Jesus and all other men come to a fulness by moving from "grace to grace" or from "gift to gift" means simply that through obedience more and more power is given by the Father until they "receive a fulness of His power [and virtue]. . . . No man is capable of perfection through his own efforts alone. A greater endowment, or gift of power, beyond man's own capabilities is required."[3] Thus, grace is an enabling power that increases our ability to become like our Heavenly Father.

Commenting on the fact that He grew to perfection, like we all need to do, President Lorenzo Snow said:

> When Jesus lay in the manger, a helpless infant, He knew not that He was the Son of God, and that formerly He created the earth. When the edict of Herod was issued, He knew nothing of it; He had not power to save Himself; and His father and mother had to take Him and fly into Egypt to preserve Him from the effects of that edict. Well, He grew up to manhood, and during His progress it was revealed unto Him who He was, and for what purpose He was in the world. The glory and power He possessed before He came into the world was made known unto Him.[4]

Elder McConkie further described Christ's childhood by saying,

> He was as much the product of the mother who bare him as were her other children. As a babe he began to grow, normally and naturally, and there was nothing supernatural about it. He learned to crawl, to walk, to run. He spoke his first word, cut his first tooth, took his first step—the same as other children do. He learned to speak; he played with toys like those of his brothers and sisters; and he played with them and with the neighbor children. He went to sleep at night and he awoke with the morning light . . .
>
> He learned to speak, to read, to write; he memorized passages of scripture, and he pondered their deep and hidden meanings. He was taught in the home by Mary, then by Joseph, as was the custom of the day. Jewish traditions and the provisions of the Torah were discussed daily in his presence. He learned the Shema, reverenced the Mezuzah, and participated in prayers, morning, noon, and night. Beginning at five or six he went to school, and certainly continued to do so until he became a son of the law at twelve years of age.[5]

THE VISIT TO THE TEMPLE

After their return from Egypt, the next recorded event in the Savior's early life was His visit to the temple in Jerusalem. Parents had the responsibility of teaching their children the law of Moses at home. The schools that all boys were required to attend were generally held in the synagogues. Until they were ten years of age, no textbooks were used except scripture. When he reached twelve, a boy in Israel was ready to commit himself to his religion and his nation's way of life by becoming a "son of the law," or in Hebrew, *Bar Mitzvah.*[6]

To become a son of the law, Jewish boys were (and still are, in many instances) taken to Jerusalem to be tested by the doctors of the law in the temple, to see if they understood their duties and privileges:

> *And when he was twelve years old, they went up to Jerusalem, after the custom, to the feast.*
>
> *And when they had fulfilled the days, as they returned, the child Jesus tarried behind, in Jerusalem; and Joseph and his mother knew not that he tarried;*
>
> *But they, supposing him to have been in the company, went a day's journey; and they sought him among his kindred and acquaintance.*
>
> *And when they found him not, they turned back again to Jerusalem, seeking him.*
>
> *And it came to pass, after three days they found him in the temple, sitting in the midst of the doctors, and they were hearing him, and asking him questions.*
>
> *And all who heard him were astonished at his understanding and answers.* (JST, Luke 2:42–47)

Only twelve years old, and Jesus was teaching the most learned men of Israel! He knew the Torah well. After all, He's the one (in His premortal state) who gave the law to Moses on Mt. Sinai (see 3 Nephi 15:5). He's the one who had spoken to all the prophets of the Old Testament "face to face" (see Exodus 33:11). He is Jehovah. And although His premortal memory was restored to Him "line upon line," by the time He was twelve years old He was prepared to teach the most learned men in the temple.

Referring to this experience, the Prophet Joseph Smith taught, "When still a boy He had all the intelligence necessary to enable Him to rule and govern the kingdom of the Jews, and could reason with the wisest and most profound doctors of law and divinity, and make their theories and practice to appear like folly compared with the wisdom He possessed; but He was a boy only, and lacked physical strength even to defend His own person; and was subject to cold, to hunger and to death."[7]

After searching for Him for three days, His parents were undoubtedly extremely worried and upset. But when they found Him in the temple they heard Him announce His mission. These are the first mortal words we have any record of Christ speaking:

> And when his parents saw him, they were amazed; and his mother said unto him, Son, why hast thou thus dealt with us? Behold, thy father [Joseph] and I have sought thee sorrowing. And he said unto them, Why is it that ye sought me? Knew ye not that I must be about my Father's business? (JST Luke 2:48–49).

His Father's business? To redeem mankind! Where did He get such incredible wisdom? He answered that question Himself during His ministry. "I do nothing of myself; but as my Father hath taught me, I speak these things" (John 8:28). "For I have not spoken of myself; but the Father which sent me, he gave me a commandment, what I should say, and what I should speak . . . whatsoever I speak therefore, even as the Father said unto me, so I speak" (John 12:49–50). No question that Joseph and Mary did the best they could to teach Jesus the gospel, but He also received training from His Father and through the whisperings of the Spirit. By the time He was twelve, He knew who He was and understood that He should be "about his Father's business." Similarly, Elder Maxwell taught, when we seek to improve ourselves at work, in school, or in our personal lives, we are doing His work: "I hope you have come, or will come, to feel that in your pursuit of higher education you are 'about your Father's business.' In today's world, equipping oneself to be an effective servant of God and mankind requires an extended educational effort."[8]

> And he spake not as other men, neither could he be taught; for he needed not that any man should teach him. (JST, Matthew 3:25)

A TIME OF PREPARATION

Jesus subjected Himself gladly and willingly to Joseph and Mary (Luke 2:51). Even as a little child, He set the example for all of us. He had brothers and sisters and was an obedient son. He grew mentally, physically, spiritually, and socially:

And Jesus increased in wisdom and stature, and in favour with God and man. (Luke 2:52)

Wisdom is the ability to anticipate consequences; it is "intelligence, or in other words, light and truth. Light and truth forsake that evil one" (D&C 93:36–37). President Ezra Taft Benson discussed how we, too, should strive to greater wisdom:

> Wisdom is the proper application of true knowledge. Not all knowledge has the same worth—nor are all truths equally valuable. The truths upon which our eternal salvation rests are the most crucial truths that we must learn. No man is truly educated unless he knows where he came from, why he is here, and where he can expect to go in the next life. He must be able to adequately answer the question Jesus posed, "What think ye of Christ?"
>
> This world cannot teach us these things. Therefore, the most essential knowledge for you to obtain is the saving knowledge of the gospel and of its Author—even Jesus Christ.
>
> Eternal life, the greatest gift that God can give and the life for which we all should be striving, comes from knowing our Father in heaven and his Son Jesus Christ. As the Savior said: "This is life eternal, that they might know thee the only true God, and Jesus Christ, whom thou hast sent." (John 17:3)[9]

As the Prophet Alma counselled his children, "O, remember . . . and learn wisdom in thy youth; yea, learn in thy youth to keep the commandments of God" (Alma 37:35).

The time eventually came for Him to begin His mortal ministry:

And after many years, the hour of his ministry drew night. (JST Matthew 3:26).

Nephi described the power and majesty with which Christ served: "I beheld the Son of God going forth among the children of men; and I saw many fall down at his feet and worship him. . . . And I beheld that he went forth ministering unto the people, in power and great glory; and the multitudes were gathered together to hear him" (1 Nephi 11:24, 28). Christmas provides the perfect setting for us to gather our families together "to hear him."

Notes

1. Alfred Edersheim, *The Life and Times of Jesus the Messiah* (Grand Rapids: William B. Eerdmans Publishing Co., 1967), 214; quoted in Robert A. Millett, "The Birth of the Messiah—a Closer Look at the Infancy Narrative of Matthew," *A Symposium on the New Testament* (Salt Lake City: The Church of Jesus Christ of Latter-day Saints, 1980), 140.

2. Joseph Smith, *The Teachings of the Prophet Joseph Smith*, 261; Jesus' statement to the Jews about Zacharias' death is found in Matthew 23:33–35.

3. *Doctrine and Covenants Student Manual—Rel. 324–325* (Salt Lake City: The Church of Jesus Christ of Latter-day Saints, 1981), 218.

4. Lorenzo Snow, in *Conference Report*, April 1901, 3.

5. Bruce R. McConkie, *The Mortal Messiah*, 1:368–69.

6. Alfred Edersheim, *The Life and Times of Jesus the Messiah,* 2 vols. (1883; reprint, New York: Longmans Green and Co., 1950), 230–32, 235.

7. Joseph Smith, *Teachings of the Prophet Joseph Smith*, 392.

8. Neal A. Maxwell, "An Evaluative Look at Today's LDS Youth," Institute of Religion devotional, Mar. 29, 1968, typescript, Church Historical Department, Salt Lake City, Utah, 1.

9. Ezra Taft Benson, "In His Steps," in *1979 Devotional Speeches of the Year* (Provo, Utah: Brigham Young University Press, 1980), 61.

SIXTEEN

WISE MEN AND WISE WOMEN

Still Seek Him

THE BABY JESUS WAS BORN in the humblest of circumstances. He lived without title to home or estate, without ambition for the things of this world, had no wardrobe but tunic and sandals, received no degrees from Alexandria or Athens, was not honored with certificates and plaques commemorating His civic service. His message was of the second mile, of returning good for evil. He bowed his back to the lash of enemies. He had no temples, monuments, castles, or tombs erected in His lifetime, yet He "has become the greatest and mightiest figure of all mankind. He was the only perfect man to walk the earth. He has become our exemplar, our teacher, our salvation, our Redeemer, our hope of eternal life."[1] And He is coming to visit us again, "for behold, verily, verily, I say unto you, the time is soon at hand that I shall come in a cloud with power and great glory" (D&C 34:7).

Like the shepherds who heralded His first coming, we know not the day nor the hour. And like the wise men who sought diligently, we are waiting and earnestly looking for the signs of His Second Coming. For "he that liveth when the Lord shall come, and hath kept the faith, blessed is he" (D&C 63:50).

At Christmastime we sing a carol that describes not the birth of the Lord, but His glorious Second Coming to the earth in the latter days. "Joy to the World" is not really a Christmas carol at all! It was written to herald the coming of the Christ and to teach us of the marvelous changes attending that event:

Joy to the world, the Lord is come;
Let earth receive her King!
Let every heart prepare him room
And Saints and angels sing.

Rejoice! Rejoice when Jesus reigns,
And Saints their songs employ,
While fields and floods, rocks, hills, and plains
Repeat the sounding joy.

No more will sin and sorrow grow,
Nor thorns infest the ground;
He'll come and make the blessings flow
Far as the curse was found.

Rejoice! Rejoice in the Most High,
While Israel spreads abroad
Like stars that glitter in the sky,
And ever worship God.

The Second Advent of Christ is drawing near. But we needn't panic. We don't need to become alarmists. Alma's attitude is a healthy one that could help us today: "And now we only wait to hear the joyful news declared unto us by the mouth of angels, of his coming; for the time cometh, we know not how soon. Would to God that it might be in my day; but let it be sooner or later, in it I will rejoice" (Alma 13:25).

The scriptures describe the Second Coming as being both a "great" and "dreadful" day. How can it be both? President Ezra Taft Benson has answered, "His coming will be both glorious and terrible, depending on the spiritual condition of those who remain."[2]

To Joseph Smith, the Lord counseled us to prepare for the "great" not the "dreadful" day: "Yea, let the cry go forth among all people: Awake and arise and go forth to meet the Bridegroom; behold and lo, the Bridegroom cometh; go ye out to meet him. *Prepare yourselves for the great day of the Lord.* Watch, therefore, for ye know neither the day nor the hour" (D&C 133:10–11; emphasis added).

President Ezra Taft Benson has testified of the choice generation to which we belong:

> For nearly six thousand years, God has held you in reserve to make your appearance in the final days before the Second Coming of the Lord.
>
> . . . While our generation will be comparable in wickedness to the days of Noah, when the Lord cleansed the earth by flood, there is a major difference this time. And that is that God has saved for the final inning some of his strongest children, who will help bear off the Kingdom triumphantly. And that is where you come in, for you are the generation that must be prepared to meet your God.
>
> All through the ages the prophets have looked down through the corridors of time to our day. Billions of the deceased and those yet to be born have their eyes on us. Make no mistake about it you are a marked generation. There has never been more expected of the faithful in such a short period of time than there is of us.[3]

Wise men and wise women still seek Him above the things of the world and the honors of men (see D&C 121:34–35). Their search will not be in vain.

> And they shall be mine, saith the Lord of hosts, in that day when I make up my jewels; and I will spare them, as a man spareth his own son that serveth him. . . . For behold, the day cometh, that shall burn as an oven; and all the proud, yea, and all that do wickedly, shall be stubble: and the day that cometh shall burn them up, saith the Lord of hosts, that it shall leave them neither root nor branch. But unto you that fear my name shall the Sun of righteousness arise with healing in his wings; and ye shall go forth, and grow up as calves of the stall. And ye shall tread down the wicked; for they shall be ashes under the soles of your feet in the day that I shall do this, saith the Lord of hosts. (Malachi 4:1–3)

The promises of the Lord are sure, but there are moments in mortality when we may doubt that the Lord's plan will work. There is nothing wrong with the plan, but the ever widening storm of darkness may cause some to wonder whether it's really worth it to keep trying to live the gospel and to keep the commandments. The Lord knew beforehand that our faith might falter. He counseled us to wait patiently. Patience is prolonged obedience. And those who trust in the Lord shall be greatly blessed (see Psalm 73 and Malachi 3:13–18).

Sometimes reading about the Second Coming scares us. "If ye are prepared ye shall not fear," the Lord said to Joseph Smith (D&C 38:30). Jedediah Morgan Grant, counselor in the First Presidency to President Brigham Young and father of President Heber J. Grant, once said, "Why is it that the Latter-day Saints are perfectly calm and serene among all the convulsions of the earth—the turmoils, strife, war, pestilence, famine and distress of nations. It is because the spirit of prophecy has made known to us that such things would actually transpire upon the earth. We understand it and view it in its true light. We have learned it by the visions of the Almighty!"[4]

STAY CLOSE TO THE SPIRIT

As he began the trek west, President Brigham Young was lying ill at the place called Winter Quarters. He was still deeply grieved at the loss of his closest earthly friend and burdened heavily with the leadership of the Kingdom. He awoke one morning and shared with some of the Brethren a dream he had in which he saw the Prophet Joseph Smith. Brigham asked Joseph if he had a message for the Saints. Joseph replied,

> Tell [them] to be humble and faithful and be sure to keep the Spirit of the Lord, that it will lead them aright. Be careful and not turn away the still small voice; it will teach them what to do and where to go; it will yield the fruits of the kingdom. Tell the brethren to keep their hearts open to conviction, so that when the Holy Ghost comes to them, their hearts will be ready to receive it. They can tell the Spirit of the Lord from all other spirits; it will whisper peace and joy to their souls, take malice, strife, and all evil from their hearts, and their whole desire will be to do good, bring forth righteousness, and build up the Kingdom of God." Over and over again the Prophet Joseph said, "Tell the people to be sure to keep the Spirit of the Lord and follow it and it will lead them just right."[5]

To help us better understand how to prepare for the Second Coming, when all of the injustices will be set right, the Savior shared three parables: the ten virgins, the talents, and the sheep and the goats (see Matthew 25). In the parable of the ten virgins, five of them were "wise" because they were prepared with an abundance of oil. The oil of the Spirit cannot be purchased at the last minute. It is accumulated one drop at a time, through kind deeds, daily prayers, unselfish service, personal sacrifice, freely given tithes and offerings, willing acceptance of callings, and so on. Wise men and wise women sincerely strive to follow the promptings of the Holy Ghost. Like the wise virgins in the parable, the Lord revealed to Joseph Smith, they do three things:

> And at that day, when I shall come in my glory, shall the parable be fulfilled which I spake concerning the ten virgins. For they that are wise and *have received the truth,* and *have taken the Holy Spirit for their guide,* and *have not been deceived*—verily I say unto you, they shall not be hewn down and cast into the fire, but shall abide the day. And the earth shall be given unto them for an inheritance; and they shall multiply and wax strong, and their children shall grow up without sin unto salvation. For the Lord shall be in their midst, and his glory shall be upon them, and he will be their king and their lawgiver. (D&C 45:56–59; emphasis added)

The Holy Ghost will place "sudden strokes of intelligence" in our minds and whisper to our hearts messages of comfort and counsel: "Yea, behold, I will tell you in your mind and in your heart, by the Holy Ghost, which shall come upon you and which shall dwell in your heart. Now, behold, this is the spirit of revelation" (D&C 8:2–3). Thoughts that "occupy" our minds, and feelings that "press themselves" upon us, are from the Lord (D&C 128:1).

Notes

1. The wording in the first part of this paragraph came from the ideas expressed in a Christmas card sent to CES employees by Stephen K. Iba, CES Area Director. The quote is from President Gordon B. Hinckley, "He Came As Babe in Manger, Not in Glory," *LDS Church News*, Dec. 7, 1991, 3–4.

2. Ezra Taft Benson, "Prepare Yourself for the Great Day of the Lord," *New Era*, May 1982, 49.

3. Ezra Taft Benson, "In His Steps," BYU Fourteen Stake Fireside, Mar. 4, 1979, in *1979 Devotional Speeches of the Year* (Provo, Utah: Brigham Young University Press, 1980), 1.

4. Jedediah Morgan Grant, "The Hand of God in Events on Earth," *Improvement Era*, vol. 18 (February 1915), 286.

5. See Brigham Young, "Chapters from the History of the Church," *Millennial Star*, vol. 35, (23 September 1873), 597–98.

SEVENTEEN

"MAYBE CHRISTMAS

Doesn't Come from a Store"

THE DEVILISH GRINCH WAS RIGHT![1] He learned in one night what it takes some a lifetime to understand—Christmas means so much more than the pretty packages and toys from tinsel town. As Elder Holland put it, "Part of the purpose for telling the story of Christmas is to remind us that Christmas doesn't come from a store. Indeed, however delightful we feel about it, even as children, each year it 'means a little bit more.' And no matter how may times we read the biblical account of that evening in Bethlehem, we always come away with a thought—or two—we haven't had before."[2]

Madison Avenue is constantly trying to convince us that we need to splurge and spend lots of money and buy lots of things in order to be happy. Peggy Noonan shared her observations about why materialism and money can't buy happiness:

> Somewhere in the Seventies, or the Sixties, we started expecting to be happy, and changed our lives (left town, left families, switched jobs) if we were not. And society strained and cracked in the storm. I think we have lost the old knowledge that happiness is overrated—that, in a way, life is overrated. We have lost, somehow, a sense of mystery—about us, our purpose, our meaning, our role. Our ancestors believed in two worlds, and understood this to be the solitary, poor, nasty, brutish and

short one. We are the first generation of man that actually expected to find happiness here on earth, and our search for it has caused such unhappiness. The reason: If you do not believe in another, higher world, if you believe only in the flat material world around you, if you believe that this is your only chance at happiness—if that is what you believe, then you are not disappointed when the world does not give you a good measure of its riches, you are despairing."[3]

Our hopes and the desires of the heart must be centered on the riches of eternal life more than the mortal messes of pottage we so often hunger for and covet. (See Genesis 25:29–34; Ether 12:4; and D&C 6:7; 14:7). Instead of asking, "What did you get *for* Christmas," perhaps we should start asking "What did you get *from* Christmas?"[4] It's so easy to let the rush of Christmas crowd out the very thing that Christmas is.[5] It helps to remember that Christmas is remarkable more for what was given than for what was received.

What makes Christmas really seem like Christmas? No one remembers the presents from one year to the next. But what we never forget are the lessons we learned, the good food, family gatherings, friendly togetherness, and above all else, the retelling of the Christmas story with a manger, stars, angelic choirs, shepherds, Joseph, Mary, and the baby Jesus. The Christmases we remember the most often have little to do with worldly goods and more to do with the spirit of caring, love, and compassion. "Christmas gifts," Elder John A. Widtsoe reminded us, "should be in memory of the divine gift, the life of Jesus Christ."[6]

"If we define our most memorable Christmases by acts of giving rather than acts of receiving, then in that same spirit we should pause and consider those around us who can benefit from our help."[7] The simplicity of the wise men's gifts stand in stark contrast to much of the materialism we experience at Christmas. The shepherds' gifts were even less worldly— they brought their love, concern, and gave their valuable time. "The difference lies in what is in the heart, not what is in the hand."[8]

In December 1911, the First Presidency (Joseph F. Smith, Anthon H. Lund, and Charles W. Penrose) reminded the Saints that having a *great* Christmas does not mean having *a lot* of things:

> Festivities on these occasions are timely and to be commended. But they should be tempered with moderation and never indulged in to excess. Let jubilation be rational and merriment be kept within proper bounds. Christmas gifts are suitable when such as the givers can reasonably bestow. The children should be made glad, the poor be

remembered, families be united, faults be forgiven, charity extended and animosities be subdued. We offer benedictions to all mankind. God bless the Saints who are under covenant to serve Him always. May His favor go forth to all nations and peoples. May the light of truth prevail against the darkness of this world, and joy and gladness chase the sorrows of troubled hearts and lift the souls of the downtrodden and the weary to heights of heavenly bliss. . . . A merry Christmas to all, bringing forth a happy and prosperous New Year![9]

A MATTER OF TIMING

One significant insight gained about gift giving from the visit of the wise men is that they came from a long distance, causing them to arrive much later than the night Christ was born. "Maybe," Elder Holland suggested, "the purchasing and the making and the wrapping and the decorating—those delightfully generous and important expressions of our love at Christmas—should be separated, if only slightly, from the more quiet, personal moments when we consider the meaning of the baby (and his birth) who prompts the giving of such gifts."[10]

THE GIFT OF PRESENCE

People universally agree that "it is more blessed to give than to receive" (Acts 20:35). But even when trying to find gifts for others, it's not uncommon to experience various degrees of anxiety and frustration looking for that perfect gift, especially for people who already have so much. Do you feel that Christmas has become too commercialized? "For some, it is a frantic, over-commercialized activity; for others, a celebration of love and selflessness, a radiation outward and upward that blesses the giver more than the receiver."[11] Perhaps, in a unique way, all of the shopping, the effort to check off the gift list, and to do it within the budgeting constraints we face, can itself bring the Christmas spirit! It requires us to turn our thoughts (and pocketbooks) to others, and away from ourselves. That's an important part of Christmas.

Have you ever noticed that our banks and shopping centers resemble ancient temples with marble floors, ornate columns, and brass? Perhaps it's because that is where we worship! Our pecuniary society has forgotten that the greatest gifts can't be purchased in stores. They are homemade, or rather "heart"-made. The most memorable family experiences at Christmastime will be those that touch the heart and enrich the spirit, not drain the pocketbook.

Ralph Waldo Emerson once wrote, "Rings and other jewels are not gifts, but apologies for gifts. The only [true] gift is a portion of thyself."[12] President Gordon B. Hinckley observed that Christmas does mean giving: "The Father gave His Son and the Son gave His life. Without giving there is no true Christmas, and without sacrifice there is no true worship."[13]

What is the most significant treasure you could give at Christmastime, or at any time? Love. It's the one gift everyone needs, everyone likes to get, and we could all use. It is easy to feel love and goodwill at Christmastime; it is much harder to do good deeds all year long. We have a great need to show more gratitude to others. We probably don't reflect often enough upon the good things in our lives. But when we do, invariably, our thoughts center around those we love. As we think about those people who mean so much to us, and for so many years have made us happy, we are grateful indeed and realize how much we love them and how much more we should say "thank you."

To make our gift giving complete, the gift of service could be added to our list. "Be thou an example of the believers," the apostle Paul taught, "in word, in conversation, in charity, in spirit, in faith, in purity" (see 1 Timothy 4:12).

Emily Smith Stuart, daughter of President George Albert Smith, recalled how her father would give of himself, even though he didn't have many worldly possessions, to see that those in need were not forgotten:

> Father always took us with him to make the rounds of the forgotten friends that he habitually visited on Christmas. I was a very little girl when I went with Father to see how the other half of the people lived. I remember going down a long alley in the middle of a city block where there were some very poor houses. We opened the door of one tiny home and there on the bed lay an old woman, very sad and alone. As we came in, tears ran down her cheeks, and she reached over to take hold of Father's hand as we gave her our little remembrances. "I am grateful to you for coming," she said, "because if you hadn't come I would have [had] no Christmas at all. No one else has remembered me." We thoroughly enjoyed this part of our day. . . .
>
> All of our holiday celebrations at Christmas were motivated by the thought impressed upon us in early childhood: "It is more blessed to give than to receive." In fact, not only Christmas, but every day of our father's life stressed this philosophy, the practicing of which made a lifelong impression upon our minds. We believe in Christmas![14]

Elder Spencer W. Kimball also spoke of the love and goodwill we can show toward others: "Christmas can be so glorious! . . . We can visit the sick, bring joy to the despairing, peace to the unfortunate, and like our Master . . . give more of ourselves and less of our assets."[15] President Kimball himself was an example of the Savior's teaching: "Whatsoever ye would that men should do to you, do ye even so to them" (Matthew 7:12). He lived this golden rule, as President Gordon B. Hinckley recounted:

> Many already know part of this story. It occurred a few years ago in the winter at O'Hare International Airport, that great and busy place that serves the city of Chicago. On this occasion a severe storm had caused delays and cancellations of flights. The thousands of people stranded or delayed there were impatient and cross and irritable. Among those in trouble was a woman, a young mother standing in a long line at the check-in counter. She had a two-year-old child who was on the dirty floor at her feet. She was pregnant with another child. She was sick and weary to the bone. Her doctor had warned her against bending and picking up anything heavy, so as she moved slowly with the line she pushed her crying and hungry child with her foot. People who saw her made critical and cutting remarks, but none offered to help.

> Then a man came toward her and with a smile of kindness on his face said, "You need help. Let me help you." He lifted the dirty, crying child from the floor and held her warmly in his arms. Taking a stick of gum from his pocket, he gave it to the child. Its sweet taste calmed her. He explained to those in the line the woman's need of help, then took her to the head of the line, spoke with the ticket agent, and soon had her checked in. He then found seats where she and her child could be comfortable, chatted for a moment, and disappeared into the crowd without giving his name. She went on her way to her home in Michigan.

> Years later there came to the office of the President of the Church a letter which reads as follows:

> "Dear President Kimball:

> "I am a student at Brigham Young University. I have just returned from my mission in Munich, West Germany. I had a lovely mission and learned much. . . .

> "I was sitting in priesthood meeting last week, when a story was told of a loving service which you performed some twenty-one years ago in the Chicago airport. The story told of how you met a young pregnant mother with a . . . screaming child, in . . . distress, waiting in a long line for her tickets. She was threatening miscarriage and therefore

couldn't lift her child to comfort her. She had experienced four previous miscarriages, which gave added reason for the doctor's orders not to bend or lift.

"You comforted the crying child and explained the dilemma to the other passengers in line. This act of love took the strain and tension off my mother. I was born a few months later in Flint, Michigan.

"I just want to *thank you* for your love. *Thank you* for your example!"[16]

There are so many people we could help: widows, students far from home, foreigners traveling through, the ill confined to homes or beds, those lingering in nursing homes, children who may not have a Christmas without the help of others, and workers who provide important services requiring them to be away from their families over the holidays.

Some creative and thoughtful gifts from the heart might include a basket of food and goodies to those on fixed incomes, lined stationery with envelopes and a generous supply of postage stamps, a box of greeting cards for all occasions for the homebound, money to those in school or living on a pension, a year's subscription to a newspaper or magazine you know they would enjoy, a gift certificate to a favorite store or car wash, or a "Twelve Days of Christmas" project with grandparents (leaving small presents or doing acts of kindness for each of the twelve days before or after Christmas).

There are also many things we can do for others, to give ourselves away—non-material gifts from the heart: an invitation to someone who is alone to spend the holiday with you and your family; reading to an older or bedridden person for an afternoon; an extra session in the temple for a truly "white" Christmas, or, better yet, preparing to take your family to the temple for the first time; repairing something; styling hair; cooking one of your specialties; driving someone who has no means of transportation to an institute class (better still, go with them!); typing a personal or family history, or a book of memories about your parents/grandparents; greeting someone with a cheery wish or meeting someone you have neglected getting to know; letters to friends you haven't seen in a long time (or to servicemen, missionaries, neglected relatives with a message of love, peace, good will, and gratitude); or a poetic verse about the family (Clement Clarke Moore wrote a poem for his children and read it to them on Christmas Eve, a poem known today by the title "The Night Before Christmas"); or visits after the holidays when lonely people tend to be forgotten so quickly.

One grandmother who received such an act of service wrote, "The week before Christmas [my daughter-in-law] came to my house with a housecleaning crew, and in four hours, two husky men and two spry little ladies cleaned my five-room house from top to bottom. My windows were washed, the oven was clean as new, and all I did was sit and watch! . . . On Christmas Day the whole family came back with a picnic-like supper and useful presents such as new dish cloths, dish towels, a pot scrubber, rubber scraper, etc. And then I felt like the best-loved grandma, mother and mother-in-law in town!"[17]

May our families feel loved this year, more because of our presence, not simply because of our presents.

DO UNTO OTHERS

What to do this Christmas? Christmas is celebration, and there is no celebration to compare with the stirring of the heart that extends itself toward the core of life—doing unto others as we would have them do to us; loving others as our own selves (see Matthew 7:12; Leviticus 19:18). An unknown author has suggested:

> Mend a quarrel. Seek out a forgotten friend. Dismiss suspicion and replace it with trust. Write a letter. Share some treasure. Give a soft answer. Encourage youth. Manifest your loyalty in word and deed. Keep a promise. Find the time. Forego a grudge. Forgive an injury. Listen. Apologize if you were wrong. Try to understand. Suppress envy. Examine your demands on others. Think first of someone else. Appreciate others. Be kind. Be gentle. Laugh a little. Laugh a little more. Deserve confidence. Take up arms against malice. Decry complacency. Express your gratitude. Have faith. Go to Church. Welcome a stranger. Gladden the heart of a child. Take pleasure in the beauty and the wonder of the earth. Speak your love. Speak it again. Speak it still once more.[18]

By sharing yourself and your talents, you leave yourself and others richer: "You cannot give yourself poor in this work," President Marion G. Romney reminded us. "You can only give yourself rich."[19] And the wonderful thing about Christmas coming each year is time and another opportunity to do something for someone. There is still time for each of us to reach out in help to others. "There are so many in distress, so many in pain, so many who walk in loneliness, whose lives we can bless, even with a small touch. This is the hour," President Hinckley declared, "to make resolution to do so."[20]

GIFTS TO THE LORD

Elder John A. Widtsoe said, "Our first gift at Christmas should be to the Lord."[21] But how do you give a gift directly to the Lord? We can give to Him *indirectly* by sharing gifts with those in need, for "when ye are in the service of your fellow beings ye are only in the service of your God" (Mosiah 2:17); and "inasmuch as ye have done it unto one of the least of these my brethren, ye have done it unto me" (Matthew 25:40).[22] But we give Him a gift *directly* through obedience, sacrifice, and love.[23] Perhaps, from an eternal perspective, the most priceless gift we can give is simply to remain true and faithful to the standards He taught (see D&C 86:10 and 78:7).

What is the most significant thing we could give? What would do the world the most good? What could really bring peace on earth and promote good will among men? Just simply remembering Him and appreciating what He did for us would help.

Elder James E. Talmage shared a parable to help us learn how important it is to appreciate and remember what the Lord has done. He tells the story of a well-read natural history professor in the nineteenth century who had been called to a grand estate in England to be honored for his contributions to the world of science. In the course of his customary daily walk, he came upon two boys at a millpond. He could also hear the frantic mewing of a cat, and so he decided to see what was happening. In a basket near the boys he could see three whining kittens; two others in the pond were struggling to keep from sinking to their doom; and the mother cat running back and forth on the bank, rampant in her distress over the drowning of her kittens. He asked the boys what they were doing. They replied that the mistress of the great estate owned and loved this mother cat, but that she didn't want any more cats around the house. She had hired them, because they were children of the servants in the estate, to go down and drown the kittens.

The naturalist assured the boys that he was a personal friend of their employer and would see that they didn't get into any trouble if he could have the remaining three kittens. To his surprise, "the mother cat evinced more than the measure of intelligence usually attributed to the animal world" by acting as if she understood exactly what was happening. She recognized him as the deliverer of her three children and rubbed his leg and purred with grateful yet mournful purrs. He took the kittens back to his cottage and gave them some milk and put them in a warm box.

The next day when all of the notable visitors were gathered to honor the scientist, the mother cat came in. In her mouth she carried a large, fat mouse, "not yet dead but struggling under the pains of torturous capture." She walked to the scientist and laid the mouse at his feet. Some in the room were repulsed, but the guest of honor probably wept.

Elder Talmage then explained,

> What think you of the offering, and the purpose that prompted the act? A live mouse, fleshy and fat! Within the cat's power of possible estimation and judgment it was a superlative gift. To her limited understanding no rational creature could feel otherwise than pleased over the present of a meaty mouse. Every sensible cat would be ravenously joyful with such an offering. Beings unable to appreciate a mouse for a meal were unknown to the cat.
>
> Are not our offerings to the Lord—our tithes and our other free-will gifts—as thoroughly unnecessary to His needs as was the mouse to the scientist? But remember that the grateful and sacrificing nature of the cat was enlarged, and in a measure sanctified, by her offering.
>
> Thanks be to God that He gages the offerings and sacrifices of His children by the standard of their physical ability and honest intent rather than by the gradation of His esteemed station. Verily He is God with us; and He both understands and accepts our motives and righteous desires. Our need to serve God is incalculably greater than His need for our service.[24]

Contemplate the gifts given on that first Christmas morn. What had more value—the gold, frankincense, and myrrh, or the reasons those gifts were given? What did those gifts do for the infant Jesus? As precious as they were, they weren't very practical gifts for a young child. But they did do something for the wise men who brought them. They enabled them to show appreciation; they allowed them to thank and remember Him in recognition of His divine mission to save us all from sin. "As the wise men of old laid at his feet gold and frankincense and myrrh, may we," Elder Stirling W. Sill once said, "present the offering of a humble heart, and adoring spirit, and an obedient will."[25]

Ponder for a moment the gift of eternal life that Christ offers to us all:

> *O how great the holiness of our God! For he knoweth all things, and there is not anything save he knows it. And he cometh into the world that he may save all . . . if they will hearken unto his voice; for behold,*

he suffereth the pains of all men, yea, the pains of every living creature, both men, women, and children, who belong to the family of Adam. (2 Nephi 9:20–21).

The Atonement may be beyond our capacity to comprehend, but it is not beyond our capacity to appreciate and pay tribute to the Father and the Son. As we contemplate and thoughtfully acknowledge the gift of eternal life offered us, the Spirit can bless us with an enlarged understanding of this marvelous gift—His life and sacrifice. Gratitude for what Christ did inspires a feeling of thankfulness within us and enlarges our capacity to show love to others. We know that we can never repay Him, that we will always be in His debt (see Mosiah 2:20–25), but we feel so much love and appreciation we want to do something. "And out of gratitude," President Gordon B. Hinckley prayed, "may we become a little kinder, a little more generous, a little more thoughtful, a little more merciful. As He came with healing in his wings, may we reach out to heal with the balm of His everlasting love."[26] This feeling of wanting to give, to be of service, to think of others, is sometimes called the spirit of Christmas. To understand the real meaning of the phrase, we need only remove the last three letters and it becomes the Spirit of Christ.[27]

SACRIFICE IS MORE SACRED THAN INCREASE

We may occasionally feel, however, that we have nothing to offer, or that our gifts will be so ineffectual, making no significant contribution to the lives of others or to the community in which we live. Our efforts may seem small and may appear to be of no great consequence but we should remember what the Lord said of Oliver Granger: "His name shall be had in sacred remembrance from generation to generation, forever and ever, saith the Lord . . . for his sacrifice shall be more sacred unto me than his increase" (D&C 117:12–13).

And even if we, as individuals, won't be able to make that big of difference in the world, when multiplied by ten thousand little things done by those who follow Christ, or by ten million little things, great things can be accomplished. "By small and simple things are great things brought to pass" (Alma 37:6).

In the doing, a certain refining influence comes into our lives. There is more of kindness, there is more of courtesy, there is more of understanding and a reaching out to help and lift and soothe and heal. "We look to Him with love as the ideal we seek to emulate," President

Hinckley said. "Our efforts are stumbling and awkward and so often result in failure because of our selfishness, our greed, our pride, our arrogance. But we try. And the world is better for our effort."[28]

May you have the merriest of Christmases and "go on your way with hearts brimming with joy for what you know about Christ."[29] His birth really is worth celebrating! It's the Centerpiece of all that's important in Christmas.

Merry Christmas and Best Wishes for an even Brighter New Year!

Notes

1. See Dr. Seuss, *How the Grinch Stole Christmas* (New York: Random House, 1957).
2. Jeffrey R. Holland, "Maybe Christmas Doesn't Come from a Store," *Ensign*, Dec. 1977, 64.
3. Peggy Noonan, "You'd Cry too if it Happened to You," *Forbes Magazine*, Sept. 14, 1992, 65. Peggy Noonan was a CBS news writer for Dan Rather and later a speechwriter for Presidents Ronald Reagan and George Bush.
4. These questions were the subject of a *LDS Church News* editorial, "Our Gifts from Christmas," Dec. 21, 1986, 16.
5. See Richard L. Evans, *From Within These Walls* (New York: Harper and Brothers, 1946), 244.
6. John A. Widtsoe, "The Gifts of Christmas," *Ensign*, Dec. 1972, 4.
7. See "The Spirit of Christmas Caring," *LDS Church News*, editorial, Dec. 3, 1990, 16.
8. See "Priceless Gifts," *LDS Church News* editorial, Dec. 17, 1988, 16.
9. Joseph F. Smith, Anthon H. Lund, and Charles W. Penrose, as cited in James R. Clark, comp., *Messages of the First Presidency of The Church of Jesus Christ of Latter-day Saints*, 1901–1915, 6 vols. (Salt Lake City: Bookcraft, 1965–1975), 4:257–58.
10. Jeffrey R. Holland, *Ensign*, Dec. 1984, 64.
11. See "Priceless Gifts," *LDS Church News*, Dec. 17, 1988, 16.
12. Ralph Waldo Emerson, *The Complete Writings of Ralph Waldo Emerson* (New York: Wm. H. Wise and Co., 1929), 286.
13. Gordon B. Hinckley, "What Shall I Do Then with Jesus Which is Called Christ?" *BYU Speeches of the Year*, Dec. 14, 1960, 3.
14. "A Story to Tell," *Inspiring Stories for Young Latter-day Saints*, Leon R.

Hartshorn, comp. (Salt Lake City: Deseret Book, 1975), 234–36.

15. Elder Spencer W. Kimball, Christmas address delivered at the Employees' Association Christmas party, Dec. 18, 1958, typescript, Church Historical Department, 3.

16. Gordon B. Hinckley, "'Do Ye Even So to Them,' " *Ensign*, Dec. 1991, 3–4.

17. From a Dear Abby column entitled "Happy Granny in Columbus, Ohio."

18. Source unknown.

19. Marion G. Romney, in Conference Report, Oct. 1980, 137.

20. Gordon B. Hinckley, Christmas Devotional, "He Came As Babe in Manger, not in Glory," *LDS Church News*, Dec. 7, 1991, 4.

21. John A. Widtsoe, "The Gifts of Christmas," *Ensign*, Dec. 1972, 4.

22. Some of my favorite thoughts about gladly giving are these:
    - "The response of the selfish will always be that there is no room in their inn" (Elder Neal A. Maxwell, *All These Things Shall Give Thee Experience*, [Salt Lake City: Deseret Book Co., 1979], 55).
    - "Like the [good] Samaritan's, every worthwhile life will involve a generous measure of giving" (Elder Marion D. Hanks, *The Gift of Self* [Salt Lake City: Bookcraft, 1974], 1).
    - "A life can never be happy that is focused inward" (Elder Robert L. Backman, *Ensign*, Nov. 1985, 13).
    - "The Christmas Spirit is the spirit of Christ that makes our hearts glow in brotherly love and friendship and prompts us to kind deeds of service" (First Presidency Christmas Message, *LDS Church News*, Dec. 21, 1986).
    - "Don't simply give—give of yourself. Don't take without taking part" (Marvin J. Ashton, in Conference Report, Apr. 1974, 50).
    - "The true test of devotion is giving of one's self" (Stephen L. Richards, in Conference Report, Apr. 1949, 141).
    - "It is not what we receive that enriches our lives, it is what we give" (Elder George Albert Smith, in Conference Report, April 1935, 46).
    - "Always at this beautiful season, we repledge ourselves to his (the Savior's) work—and invite all people everywhere to join us in our prayers of joy and love and gratitude for the life and teachings of our Lord and Savior, Jesus Christ, the Son of God" (Spencer W. Kimball, *Ensign*, Dec. 1980, 9).
    - "The compass of the spirit of Christmas points constantly

toward others, never toward ourselves" (Hugh B. Brown, *Improvement Era*, Dec. 1970, 144).

- "Give to your enemy forgiveness, to your opponent tolerance, to your friend your heart, . . . to all men charity, to every child a good example, and to yourself respect" (Sterling W. Sill, *Christmas Sermons*, [Salt Lake City: Deseret Book, 1973], 56).

- "To give our time and self for the good of others is more important than giving material things in life" (Elder Adney Y. Komatsu, *Ensign*, November 1975, 90).

- "The happiest people I know are those who lose themselves in the service of others" (Elder Gordon B. Hinckley, *BYU Speeches of the Year,* 1977, 45).

23. See Elder John A. Widtsoe, *Improvement Era*, Dec. 1935, 752; as reprinted in "The Gifts of Christmas," *Ensign*, Dec. 1972, 4.

24. James E. Talmage, "The Parable of the Grateful Cat," *Improvement Era*, 19:875–76, Aug. 1916.

25. Source unknown.

26. Gordon B. Hinckley, "He Came As Babe," *LDS Church News*, Dec. 7, 1991, 4.

27. "The Quality of Generosity," *Relief Society Courses of Study 1977– 1978* (Salt Lake City: The Church of Jesus Christ of Latter-day Saints, 1977), 18.

28. Gordon B. Hinckley, "He Came as a Babe in a Manger, Not in Glory" *LDS Church News*, Dec. 7, 1991, 4.

29. From Elder Neal A. Maxwell's unpublished Christmas devotional to LDSSA students in Symphony Hall, Salt Lake City, Utah, Dec. 1991.

APPENDIX

A Family Christmas Nativity

If you have young children, consider having them reenact the Nativity using the following script and accompanying hymns.

Shepherd 1 (to the other shepherds)

Since the beginning of time, prophets have known and foretold the birth of Christ. Isaiah said, "Therefore, the Lord himself shall give you a sign—Behold, a virgin shall conceive, and shall bear a son, and shall call his name Immanuel.

"For unto us a child is born, unto us a son is given; and the government shall be upon his shoulder; and his name shall be called Wonderful, Counselor, The Mighty God, The Everlasting Father, The Prince of Peace."

Musical Number: "Far, Far Away on Judea's Plains" (*Hymns*, no. 212)

Far, far away on Judea's plains, Shepherds of old heard the joyous strains:

Glory to God, Glory to God, Glory to God in the highest.

Peace on earth, good will to men; Peace on earth, good will to men.

Lord, with the angels we too would rejoice; Help us to sing with the heart and voice:

Glory to God, Glory to God, Glory to God in the highest.

Peace on earth, good will to men; Peace on earth, good will to men.

153

Mary (to Joseph)

The angel Gabriel appeared unto me. He said, "Hail, thou virgin, who art highly favored of the Lord. The Lord is with thee, for thou art chosen and blessed among women." I was initially worried because I didn't understand what he was saying or what he meant by this. But then he told me, "Fear not, Mary, for thou hast found favor with God. And behold, thou shalt conceive, and bring forth a son, and shall call his name Jesus."

After he said that, I wanted to raise my voice in praise to God, just like the angels.

Musical Number: "Hark! The Herald Angels Sing" (*Hymns,* no. 209)

Hark! The herald angels sing Glory to the newborn King!
Peace on earth and mercy mild, God and sinners reconciled.
Joyful, all ye nations, rise; Join the triumph of the skies;
With th'angelic host proclaim Christ is born in Bethlehem!
Hark! The herald angels sing Glory to the newborn King!

Hail! The heav'n born Prince of peace! Hail! The Son of
*   Righteousness!*
Light and life to all he brings, Ris'n with healing in his wings.
Mild he lays his glory by, Born that man no more may die;
Born to raise the Sons of earth, Born to give them second birth.
Hark! The herald angels sing Glory to the newborn King!

Joseph

It came to pass in those days, that there went out a decree from Caesar Augustus, that all his empire should be taxed. And all went to be taxed, everyone to his own city. Since my family line is through the lineage of David and comes from Bethlehem, I needed to go there to be taxed. So, I loaded up my donkey and my very pregnant espoused wife, Mary, and we went to Bethlehem to be counted and taxed.

Musical Number: "When Joseph Went to Bethlehem" (*Children's Songbook,* 38)

When Joseph went to Bethlehem, I think he took great care
To place his tools and close his shop and leave no shavings there.
He urged the donkey forward then, with Mary on its back,

And carried bread and goat cheese in a little linen sack.
I think there at the busy inn that he was meek and mild
And awed to be the guardian of Mary's sacred child.
Perhaps all through the chilly hours he smoothed the swaddling bands,
And Jesus felt the quiet strength of Joseph's gentle hands.

Joseph

And Mary brought forth her firstborn son, and wrapped him in swaddling clothes, and laid him in a manger, because there was no room for us in the inn. As I watched the baby, I remembered the prophecies that said the Son of God would be born in the most humble of circumstances and I was happy to be a part of the experience.

Musical Number: "Away in a Manger" (*Hymns,* no. 206)

Away in a manger, no crib for his bed,
The little Lord Jesus laid down his sweet head;
The stars in the heavens looked down where he lay,
The little Lord Jesus, asleep on the hay.

The cattle are lowing; the poor baby wakes,
But little Lord Jesus, no crying he makes.
I love thee, Lord Jesus; look down from the sky
And stay by my cradle till morning is nigh.

Shepherd 2

It was just another quiet, peaceful night of watching over the sheep, when suddenly there was a great light in the sky—an angel appeared unto me and my fellow shepherds. We were very afraid because we'd never seen anything like this before. The angel said, "Fear not, for behold, I bring you good tidings of great joy, which shall be to all people. For unto you is born this day, in the city of David, a Savior, who is Christ the Lord.

"And this is the way you shall find the babe, he is wrapped in swaddling clothes, and is lying in a manger." After he was done speaking, other angels appeared—it was a like a great heavenly host. And they were all praising God and saying, "Glory to God in the highest; and on earth peace; goodwill to men."

Musical Number: "Angels We Have Heard on High" (*Hymns,* no. 203)

Angels we have heard on high Sweetly singing o'er the plains,
And the mountains in reply Echoing their joyous strains.
Gloria in excelsis Deo. Gloria in excelsis Deo.

Shepherds, why this jubilee? Why your joyous strains prolong?
What the gladsome tidings be Which inspire your heav'nly song?
Gloria in excelsis Deo. Gloria in excelsis Deo.

Wise Man 1

We saw a star in the east and knew that the sign had been given that the Son of God was born. We wanted to come and worship the King, so we traveled for many days until we came to Jerusalem. On the way, we went to ask King Herod if he knew where the King of the Jews had been born. He sent us to Bethlehem to find the child and he wanted us to return, once we had found him, and tell him where Christ had been born so that he could come and worship as well.

Wise Man 2

We followed the star to Bethlehem, until it came and stood over where the young child was. When we saw the star we rejoiced because we knew that we had found the King of the Jews. We came into the house and saw the young child with Mary his mother, and fell down and worshipped him. We brought him precious gifts of gold, frankincense, and myrrh.

Wise Man 3

Being warned by God in a dream about the evil intentions of King Herod, we decided to leave by another way and not tell King Herod where to find the child. We felt honored to have the opportunity to have knelt at the feet of the King of the Jews and to worship him in such a manner during our lifetimes.

Musical Number: "With Wondering Awe" (*Hymns,* no. 210)

With wond'ring awe the wise men saw The star in heaven springing,
And with delight, in peaceful night, They heard the angels singing:
Hosanna, hosanna, hosanna to his name!

By light of star they traveled far To seek the lowly manger,
A humble bed wherein was laid The wondrous little Stranger.
Hosanna, hosanna, hosanna to his name!

Mary

Jesus Christ at the center of Christmas, just as He is at the center of our Heavenly Father's plan of happiness. One of the joys of Christmas is that it is a time when people think more of others than of themselves and all are caught up in the joy of giving. Christmas is not about who comes down the chimney, but Who came down from heaven to give us the greatest of all gifts—eternal life.

Musical Number: "Silent Night" (*Hymns,* no. 204)

Silent night! Holy night! All is calm, all is bright
Round yon virgin mother and Child. Holy Infant, so tender and mild,
Sleep in heavenly peace; Sleep in heavenly peace.

Silent night! Holy night! Shepherds quake at the sight!
Glories stream from heaven afar; Heav'nly hosts sing Alleluia!
Christ, the Savior, is born! Christ, the Savior, is born!

Silent night! Holy night! Son of God, love's pure light
Radiant beams from thy holy face, With the dawn of redeeming grace,
Jesus, Lord, at thy birth; Jesus, Lord, at thy birth.

All Together

Merry Christmas to all, and to all, an even greater New Year!

INDEX

A

Adam and Eve, fall allowed men to come to earth, 29
first to hear prophecy of Christ, 28
forgiven for fall, 30–31
Alma, testifies of Christ's empathy, 37
Angels, 104, 106
Anna, lived to see Christ, 118
Apollo 13 story, 52

B

Ballard, Melvin J., miracle of Christ's birth, 64
Benjamin, King, foresees Christ's miracles, 36
Benson, Ezra Taft, all prophets have known of Christ and His mission, 37

Book of Mormon written for our day, 49
choice generation reserved for Second Coming, 135
Christ changes human nature, 26
Christ's central role in existence, 6
Second Coming both glorious and terrible, 134
testimony of Christ, 39
Wisdom is proper application of knowledge, 131
Bethlehem, Christmas crowds remind of, 100
journey of Joseph and Mary to, 84–85
making a modern symbolic journey to, 14, 23–24, 111–12
significance of name, 85
Burton, Theodore M., priesthood rights and responsibilities, 117

C

Christmas, can help children
  distinguish between good and
  evil, 21–22
cannot be bought from a store,
  21–22
childlike faith will help one
  enjoy, 17–18
Christ is the center of, 39
finding time for God during, 85
giving secular activities their
  proper place during, 22
making Christmas visits, 143–45
mature appreciation of, 15–17
most memorable activities
  during, 140
overcoming adult emptiness
  during, 15–17, 23–24
provides opportunity to change,
  15
three levels of, 15
time to come unto Christ, 8–9
time to focus on Christ, 24
time to help those in need, 142–45
time to love others as self, 145
Christmas carols, 105
Christmas symbols
  can be part of honoring Jesus
    Christ, 21–23
  inevitable part of modern
    Christmas, 21
  may focus hearts on temporal
    things, 19–20
  may lead away from things of
    eternal value, 19
  spiritual meanings of, 18–22
Church, exists to testify of Christ,
  10–11
invites all men to come to
  Christ, 116–17
Church News, identity of wise
  men, 119–20
three levels of Christmas, 16–17
Clark, J. Reuben, Jr., Christ pro-
  claims peace of righteousness,
  106–7
magnificence of the Creator, 92

E

Edersheim, Alfred, Herod's
  slaughter of children under age
  two, 126
Egypt, holy family flees to, 127
Elizabeth, 57–59
  Mary's visit to, 76–77
Emerson, Ralph Waldo, 142
Enoch, sees Christ's life in vision,
  30–31

F

Faith, all should have childlike,
  17–18
blessing that result from, 8
definition of, 8
first principle of gospel, 7
First Presidency, 106
focusing on Christ during
  Christmas, 24
temper festivities with modera-
  tion, 140
testimony of, 64
Frankincense, 122

G

Gabriel, appears to Mary, 63–64,
    66–67
    appears to Zacharias, 57–58
    See also Noah
Gifts, best cannot be bought,
    141–45
    cat who gave mouse, 146–47
    choosing can be frustrating, 141
    even small ones significant, 148
    gift giving and reflection on
        Christ, 141
    ideas, 144–45
    love is the greatest gift, 142
    of love and goodwill, 142–43
    of service, 144–45
    to the Lord, 122–23, 146, 148
Giving, blessings of, 147
    boy gives shoes to woman, 9
    gratitude for Atonement
        inspires, 148
    more important than receiving,
        140–41
    one received back what one
        gives, 145
Grace, definition of, 128
Grant, Jedediah Morgan, Saints
    calm among convulsions of
    earth, 136

H

Handel, George Frederick, *Mes-
    siah*, 43–44
Herod, 55–56
    first foreign ruler of Palestine,
    55

slaughter of children under age
    two, 121
Hinckley, Gordon B., Christmas
    is time to help those in need,
    143–44
    Father and Son give true gifts of
        Christmas, 142
    few believed in Christ's divin-
        ity, 7
    giving helps one grow, 148
    gratitude for Atonement inspires
        love, 148
Holland, Jeffrey R., drama of
    Christ's birth, 96–97
    gift giving and reflection on
        Christ, 141
    something new learned each
        time Christmas story read,
        139
Hunter, Howard W., Christ must
    be taken into one's life, 7
    find time at Christmas for God,
    85

I

"I Heard the Bells on Christmas
    Day" (song), 108–9
Inn, description of, 98–99
    Joseph and Mary turned away
        from, 95, 99–100
Isaiah, writings of, 41–44
    correct translation of, 42
    Handel's *Messiah*, 42–43
    how Christ and the Father are
        one, 42
Israel, priests in Zacharias's time,
    57

J

Jesus Christ, ability to atone, 64–65
  as Creator, 99–100
  as shepherd, 102
  birth in humble circumstances, 95
  centerpiece of Christmas and life, 5, 27
  changes lives, 14–15
  childhood and adolescence, 125–31
  date of birth, 93
  descended below all things, 37, 96–97
  earth had greatest need of, 97
  gaining knowledge and understanding of, 7, 39
  gaining personal testimony of, genealogy of, 6, 120–21
gradually learned of His mission, 127–28
  grew from "grace to grace," 127–28
  had to be both human and divine, 65
  had to experience earth life, 96–97
  having hope and faith in, 7–8
  lawful successor to Jewish nation, 68–69
  "light to lighten the Gentiles," 116
  miracle of conception, 64
  mission of, 10–11
  must be born in one's heart, 100
  "new David," 66

only way to eternal life, 11
  overcame fall of Adam and Eve, 30
  premortal life, 39, 95
  prophecies of Him misunderstood, 38–39
  raised in normal and natural way, 128
  redeemed as infant according to Jewish law, 115–16
  showing gratitude for, 148
  significance of name, 37, 63, 83, 104
  some doubt divinity of, 7
  Son of God and Son of Man, 64, 70–71
  standing as witness, 7
  taught by the Spirit, 131
  taught learned men in temple, 129–30
  volunteered to be Savior, 105
  will crush Satan completely, 28
  wise men and women still seek, 133–37
John the Baptist, birth and naming of, 78
  birth foretold, 58
  leaps in womb, 76
  mission of, 58
  ordained to prepare way for Christ, 78
  raised in wilderness, 79
Jordan River Temple, great lights in sky accompanied dedication of, 46
Joseph, feelings about Annunciation, 81–83
  feelings at Christ's birth, 97
"Joy to the World" (song), 134

K

Kimball, Heber C., men cannot stand on borrowed light, 121
Kimball, Spencer W., giving love and goodwill at Christmas, 143
need to follow living as well as ancient prophets, 51

L

Lee, Harold B., Apollo 13 and following the prophets, 52
people need listening ears, 49
Lehi, prophesied of Christ, 34–35
Longfellow, Henry Wadsworth, 108
Luke, may have met Mary, 112
Luke 2, Christmas story in, 112
Lund, Gerald N., Christ is God first, human second, 70
description of inn, 98–99

M

Magi, *See* Wise men
Mahonri Moriancumer, talked with the Lord face to face, 32
Manger, 98
Mary, divine character of, 97–98
feelings at Christ's birth, 97–98
foreordained role of, 67
Gabriel's appearance to, 63–67
"kept all these things in her heart," 112
virgin birth of Jesus, 65, 67–68
visit to Elizabeth, 76–77

Maxwell, Neal A., Brethren will guide Church members through special challenges, 52–53
differing genealogies of Christ in New Testament, 69
education is part of doing God's will, 130
Christ's willingness to sacrifice life, 105
no room for Christ in the "inn–telect" of many, 6–7
who one is, not what one has done, will matter in the end, 20
McConkie, Bruce R., appropriateness of Gabriel's role as a messenger, 59
Christ had normal childhood, condescension of Christ, 128
earth the planet with greatest need for Christ, 96–97
how Christ spoke with Nephi night before birth, 90
John began testifying of Christ before His birth, 76–77
Mary's divine role, 67–68
three wise men, 120
McKay, David O., what one thinks of Christ determines who one is, 14
Micah, prophesies of Christ, 34
Millet, Robert L., women named in Christ's genealogy, 69
Monson, Thomas S., many still have no room for Christ, 99
Moses, prophesied of Christ, 33–34
Myrrh, 122

N

Nazareth, 127

Nephi, prophesies of Christ,
receives words from Christ the
night before His birth, 35–36

Noah, as Gabriel, 32
knew of Savior's mission, 31–32

Noonan, Peggy, money cannot
buy happiness, 139–40

O

"O Little Town of Bethlehem"
(song), 92

Ordinances and sacred ceremonies, 22–23

P

Packer, Boyd K., believing is
seeing, 17
special spirit of Christmas, 15

Passover, 22
replaced by sacrament, 34
symbolic of Atonement, 33–34

Peace, 106–11
comes through living the
gospel, 110–11
world's way versus Christ's way,
107

Peterson, Mark E., Restoration
resolved mystery of Christ's
birth, 4

Prophecies, all have testified of
Christ, 38–39
following means reading their
words, 51

listening ears for, 49
modern are as important as
ancient, 51
rejected by the worldly, 47–50

R

Romney, Marion G., Isaiah
revised without inspiration, 42
"you can only give yourself
rich," 145

S

Samuel, explains purpose of
prophecies, 47
prophesies of signs to accompany Christ's birth, 45–53
rejected by majority of people,
49, 87

Santa Claus, spiritual meaning of,
18–19

Saviors on Mount Zion, duties of,
116

Scriptures, can open eyes of
understanding, 18
main source of information
about Jesus Christ, 6
reading Christmas story with
new life, 23–24

Second Coming, and parable of
ten virgins, 136–37
and staying close to the Spirit,
136
both glorious and terrible, 134
choice generation will see, 134
Christ's first coming as a type
of, 50

"Joy to the World," 134
need not be time of fear, 134,
136
people will fall to earth, 91
signs will be reasoned away, 92
waiting for requires patience,
135–36
Shepherds, acted on angels' visit,
111–12
bore testimony of Christ, 11
"came with haste," 111
watched lambs destined for
sacrifice, 103–4
Signs and wonders, orchestrated
by Jesus Christ, 90–91
reasoning away of, 46, 76, 92
remorse of the unbelieving
when they come, 51
wicked don't believe, 87
Signs of Christ's birth, completely
fulfilled, 91
"great lights in heaven," 46
in Americas, 75, 89–90
new star, 47
night without darkness, 90
Samuels' prophecies of, 45–53
Signs, seeking of, 59–61
Still, Sterling W., giving gifts as
wise men did, 147
Simeon, 116, 118
foretold of Christ's mission, 118
Smith, George Albert, daughter's
story of making Christmas visits
men asking for signs, 142
Smith, Joseph, appearance to
Brigham Young in dream, 136
Christ ready at young age to
fulfill mission, 130–31

every man who has calling was
ordained in premortality, 83
preacher asks for signs, 60–61
signs of Second Coming will be
reasoned away, 91
three things necessary to have
faith in God, 7–8
Zacharias slain to save John's
life, 126
Snow, Lorenzo, Christ's spiritual
growth as a youth, 128
Spirit, Joseph Smith urges Brethren to keep, 137
Stable, 98–99
Stapley, Delbert L., wickedness
before Christ's birth like wickedness before Second Coming,
88
Star, 47, 90–91
bears witness of Creator, 91
not everyone saw, 122
Stuart, Emily Smith, 142
Swaddling clothes, 98
Symbols, both conceal and reveal
truth, 38
cannot be understood by hard-
hearted, 38
found abundantly in scriptures,
22
See also Christmas symbols

T

Talmage, James E., Christ had to
be both human and divine, 65
Christ was lawful successor to
Jewish nation, 69
Christ's birth date, 93

Joseph's reaction to Mary's
conception, 82
King Herod's character, 56
Roman census, 84
value of gift determined by
intent of heart, 146–47
Taxing, explanation of,
Taylor, Henry D., every Church
member can have knowledge of
God, 120–21
Taylor, John, Saints promote
peace, 107
Temple, symbolism of astrological
inscriptions on, 120

Christmas symbols, 19
Wisdom, definition of, 131
Wise men, 119–123
arrived after Christ's birth, 119
bore witness of Christ, 120
did not return to Herod, 123
gifts of, 122
identity of, 119–20

Y

Young, Brigham, sees Joseph
Smith in dream, 136

Z

Zacharias, 56–61
angel announces Elizabeth will
bear son, 58
died to save son's life, 126
prophesies of son and Jesus
Christ, 78–79
seeks sign and struck dumb,
59–61

W

Welch, Jay, on Handel's *Messiah*,
43–44
Widtsoe, John A., first gift should
be to Lord, 146
gifts should be in memory of
Christ, 140
spiritual meaning behind most

W. JEFFREY MARSH

Jeffrey Marsh is an associate professor of ancient scripture at Brigham Young University. He is the author of several books, including *The Eyewitness History of the Church* series and *Joseph Smith—Prophet of the Restoration*. He and his wife, Kathie, have conducted travel-study tours of LDS Church history sites, American history sites, Holy Land sites, and the lands of the Book of Mormon. He received a bachelor's degree from the University of Utah, and master's and doctorate degrees from Brigham Young University.